What?
No Onions!

Everyday recipes from the

FODMAP
Kitchen

BY

CHERYL BAYLIS

Grosvenor House
Publishing Limited

The right of Cheryl Baylis to be identified as the author of this
work has been asserted in accordance with Section 78
of the Copyright, Designs and Patents Act 1988

The book cover picture is copyright to Cheryl Baylis

This book is published by
Grosvenor House Publishing Ltd
Link House
140 The Broadway, Tolworth, Surrey, KT6 7Ht.
www.grosvenorhousepublishing.co.uk

A CIP record for this book
is available from the British Library

ISBN 978-1-78148-998-7

For my son Chris.

So low FODMAP Foods develop recipes to help reduce the intake of FODMAPs (Fermentable Oligo-saccharides, Di-saccharides, Mono-saccharides and Polyols).

Food contains many elements, including proteins, minerals, vitamins and carbohydrates. FODMAPs are carbohydrate sugars that are poorly absorbed; many FODMAPs are poorly absorbed in all people, but not everyone suffers from symptoms. Common poorly absorbed FODMAPs contain excess FRUCTOSE, found in some fruits and vegetables; LACTOSE, found in dairy products; SUGAR POLYOLS-SORBITOL and MANNITOL, found in some fruits, vegetables, and artificial sweeteners, and FRUCTANTS &/OR GOS, found in some fruits and vegetables, cereals/breads/snacks, drinks and supplements, nuts and seeds.

When food enters the small intestine and the FODMAPs are not absorbed, there can be an increase of water through the bowel, causing diarrhoea for some. Moving through the digestive tract to the large intestine, these carbohydrate sugars ferment with the gut bacteria. This fermentation (which can also flow back up to the small intestine) can cause irritation in the gut with symptoms such as bloating and distension, stomach cramps, constipation, and flatulence. These are typical symptoms of a condition commonly called IBS (Irritable Bowel Syndrome) and can vary in degrees, affecting one in seven adults.

Severe symptoms should always be checked out with your GP, as there may be an underlying condition that needs treating; testing can be carried out for food allergies and sometimes will result in a referral to a dietician.

Research into FODMAPs began at Monash University, Melbourne, Australia, led by Professor Peter Gibson. This research provides evidence that lowering FODMAPs in the diet can improve IBS symptoms. Further information can be found at the Monash University website for Low FODMAP diet for Irritable Bowel Syndrome

http://www.med.monash.edu/cecs/gastro/fodmap/

Those with severe symptoms may be referred to a dietician, who will likely recommend a diet involving a few weeks of strict restriction of FODMAPs followed by professional advice as to which foods (and how much) can be reintroduced. The dietician will ensure that you maintain a healthy, balanced diet.

This is not a 'fad' diet, nor is it a diet aimed at weight loss. It is a means of controlling symptoms that are uncomfortable and, for some, cause uncompromising restrictions to their lifestyle.

If your symptoms are mild and intermittent, but still disrupt your lifestyle, you may find that adjusting your homemade recipes to use low FODMAP ingredients helps to ease the bloating, excess wind, and stomach discomfort.

Unless you have malabsorption of a specific group or groups of FODMAPs, or food allergies, for example gluten/dairy intolerance, determined by medical testing, research shows that small quantities of some foods containing high FODMAPS may be tolerated. The diet should be used according to the individual and personal tolerance.

Why did I develop So Low FODMAP Foods?

Here is my personal journey into believing lowering FODMAPs in your diet can help reduce such symptoms.

My son has Duchenne Muscular Dystrophy (information about this condition can be found at the Muscular Dystrophy website: (www.musculardystrophyuk.org/app/uploads/2015/05/DMD-factsheet.pdf)

A few years ago, he began to suffer from bloating and abdominal distension that became so severe that it affected his breathing. This was due to the excess gas in his gut, creating pressure under the diaphragm. Due to the muscle weakness in his chest, this pressure made it difficult for him to expand his lungs.

After several hospital admissions, we were introduced to a gastroenterologist who suggested a low FODMAP diet. With his explanation that my son's digestive system was probably slower than normal and food was remaining in the gut longer, the slow movement of food was probably causing a longer fermentation period, thus creating a greater build-up of gas. We followed his advice and turned to the Low FODMAP diet.

Some research within Duchenne Muscular Dystrophy (DMD) has shown that there is evidence that the smooth muscle tissue of the digestive tract can become affected by fibrosis (Barohn et al. 1988). This hinders the flow of food, slowing digestion and may cause distension. Unfortunately, bloating and excess gas is only just becoming recognised as a problem with young men with DMD. Following my son's experience, his consultant now discusses these issues with all his patients.

It has not been an easy adaptation; it is very difficult to buy ready-made foods that are low FODMAP and shopping takes much longer as I have to check every package for the ingredients. At first, it felt like enjoying our favourite foods was no longer an option.

Since I enjoy cooking, I decided to dedicate my time to adapting recipes so we could, as a family, enjoy our usual favourite meals, like curries, pizza, and pasta, to mention just a few! Using the Low FODMAP diet food guide, it is possible to transform your diet and improve your symptoms.

I truly believe this diet has had a profound effect on reducing the bloating, distension and constipation that from which my son previously suffered. My mission is to promote the reduction of FODMAPs for anyone who suffers similar symptoms, whether diagnosed with IBS, DMD, or suffering from any other digestion related condition.

As a mother and not a medic, I recommend that anyone suffering such symptoms seek advice from their doctor or qualified dietician; however my recipes replace the high FODMAPs with alternative ingredients with lower FODMAPs and may help to reduce symptoms.

Index

Illustrations

Family Feasts

Tomato Soup

Ingredients   Serves 2

1 tsp vegetable oil
½ bunch spring onion greens, finely chopped
500g passata
250 ml semi-skimmed, lactose-free milk
1 Knorr Ham stock cube
1 tbsp tomato puree
2 tbsp white wine vinegar
2 tps sugar
1 bay leaf
½ tsp dried basil
Salt and pepper
125 ml lactose-free cream

Heat the oil in a large saucepan and add the herbs and the spring onion greens. Fry until the onions greens are soft.

Add the passata and slowly pour in the milk. Stir in the tomato puree, sugar, and white wine vinegar. Crumble the stock cube in and stir well. Bring to a gentle boil.

Reduce the heat and simmer for 20 minutes.

Stir in the cream and serve.

Chicken Soup

Ingredients   Serves 4

1 tbsp garlic infused olive oil
½ bunch spring onion greens, finely chopped
1 carrot, finely grated
1tsp dried thyme
1.5ltr/2pts chicken stock
275g/10oz leftover chicken, shredded (no skin)
3tbsp lactose-free natural yoghurt

50 / 2 floz. lactose-free cream

Heat the oil in a large saucepan and add the spring onion greens, carrot, and thyme. Fry until the onions greens are soft. Add the stock, stir and bring to the boil.

Lower the heat for a gentle simmer and add the shredded chicken. Simmer for 5-10 minutes.

Slowly pour in the yoghurt, stir through, and transfer to warm serving bowls. Swirl the cream on top and serve.

Cottage Pie

Ingredients   Serves 4-6

1 tsp garlic infused oil or vegetable oil
1 bunch spring onion greens, chopped
500g/1 lb minced beef
2 tsp Bovril
1 grated or diced carrot
125g/4oz frozen peas
1 tsp mixed herbs
1 tbsp tomato puree
200ml/7floz water
Salt and pepper
1 tbsp Mc Dougal's Thickening Granules (or mix1tblsp cornflour with 2tblsp of the water)

4 large potatoes, cooked and mashed with a knob of butter

Pre-heat the oven to Gas Mark 5/190 C

Heat the oil in a saucepan and stir-fry the spring onion greens until soft. Add the mince and continue stirring for 2-3 minutes until the meat is brown all over.

Add the carrots, peas, and herbs and continue cooking and stirring for another 2 minutes; then add the remaining ingredients. Stir to mix and bring to the boil, lower the heat and simmer for 5 minutes.

Transfer to an ovenproof dish and top with the mashed potato. Place in the oven and bake for 20-25 minutes, until the potato is golden.

Optional: Add some grated cheese on top before putting in the oven.
Alternatively, simmer the meat for 20-25 minutes, cover with the mashed potatoes,
then pop under a hot grill until the cheese is melted and golden.

Beef Stew

Ingredients   Serves 4

500g /1lb stewing steak
1 bunch spring onion greens, finely chopped
2 tbsp gluten-free plain flour
1 bouquet garni
550ml /1pt beef stock
1 tsp Bovril
2 tbsp garlic infused oil
1 carrot, sliced
1 leek – green part only
1 turnip, diced
Salt and pepper

Heat the oil and fry the spring onion greens to soften. Remove from the pan with a slotted spoon and set aside.

Add the beef to the hot oil and stir-fry until the beef is brown. Stir in the flour to coat the meat well and cook for another minute.

Pour in the stock, stirring constantly. Bring to the boil, add the vegetables, bouquet garni and Bovril, then lower the heat and leave to simmer gently for 2½ -3 hours. Stir occasionally.

Add dumplings for a finishing touch approximately ½hr before the end of cooking.

Beef Burger

Ingredients   Makes 6

750g beef mince
1½ tsp Bovril
1½ tsp tomato puree
1 beaten egg
1½ tsp mixed herbs
Salt and pepper
3 tbsp spring onion greens, finely chopped (or ½ tsp asafoetida)
1 tsp garlic infused oil (optional)

Mix all ingredients together until well combined.

Divide the mixture into 6 balls. Using the flat of your hand, gently squash the 'ball' into a patty shape, approximately 1 cm thick.

Set aside on a plate. When all burgers are made, place the plate in the fridge to rest for 30 minutes.

Gently fry on a pre-heated griddle pan for 3-4 minutes each side or until cooked through.

These can be frozen raw. Wrap the burgers individually in cling film or divide with wax paper circles.
This makes it easier to get them out of the freezer when required.

Chilli Con Carne

Ingredients   Serves 4-6

500g Beef mince
1 bunch spring onion greens, chopped
2tsp garlic infused oil
1 fresh chilli, finely chopped
1 tsp Bovril
½ tsp cumin
1tsp paprika
500g passata/1 can chopped tinned tomatoes
2tsp soft brown sugar
Salt and pepper

Heat the oil in a large saucepan; fry the spring onion greens and fresh chilli for a few minutes, then add the beef mince. Stir to break up the meat and fry until browned. Add the remaining ingredients and season to taste.

Bring to the boil and reduce the heat to a gentle simmer. Cook for 30-40 minutes, stirring occasionally to make sure the meat is not sticking to the bottom of the pan.

For a milder chilli, remove the pith and seeds from the fresh chilli.

Add more for a hotter one!!

Beef Bourguignon

Ingredients   Serves 4 - 6

500g diced casserole beef
200g diced smoked streaky bacon
1 bunch spring onion greens, finely chopped
275ml /½ pt red wine
2 tbsp gluten-free plain flour
1 bouquet garni
275ml /½ pt beef stock
1 tsp Bovril
2 tbsp garlic infused oil
Salt and pepper

Heat the oil and fry the spring onion greens to soften. Remove from the pan with a slotted spoon and set aside.

Add the beef and bacon to the hot oil and stir fry until the beef is brown. Stir in the flour to coat the meat well and cook for another minute.

Pour in the red wine, stirring constantly. Bring to the boil then lower the heat and simmer for 5 minutes.

Add the bouquet garni, Bovril, spring onion greens and stock. Season and stir. Lower the temperature and place a lid on the saucepan (or cover with foil). Leave to simmer gently for 3 hours.

Don't be tempted to use cheap wine…find a decent one on offer!

Beef and Bacon Meatloaf

Ingredients   Serves 6

500g /1lb beef mince
300g /12oz smoked bacon, chopped
1 tbsp garlic infused oil (and a little more for greasing the loaf tin)
1 bunch spring onion greens, finely chopped
50g /2oz fresh gluten-free breadcrumbs
1 tsp smoked paprika
1 tbsp finely chopped fresh basil
1 egg, beaten
Salt and pepper
2 tbsp onion jam (optional)

Pre-heat the oven to Gas 6/200C.

Heat the oil and fry the bacon and spring onion greens for 2 minutes in a large saucepan.

Remove from the heat and add the remaining ingredients. Mix well to ensure all ingredients are well combined.

Grease a 450g /1lb loaf tin with garlic infused oil. Fill with the meat mixture, pressing down firmly. Top with a layer of onion jam, if using. Cover with foil.

Place the loaf tin on a baking tray and bake in the oven for 35-40 minutes. Remove the foil for the last 10 minutes.

Serve with Tomato Chutney

Stuffed Marrow

Ingredients   Serves 4

1 large marrow (or over grown courgette)
1 tsp garlic infused oil
1 bunch spring onion greens, chopped
1 fresh, deseeded chilli, finely chopped
400g/14oz minced lamb
1 tsp ground cumin seeds
1 tsp ground coriander seeds
½ tsp cinnamon
2 tblsp fresh coriander leaf, chopped
150ml/5floz passata
150ml/5floz lamb stock
75g/3oz sultanas (optional)
Salt and pepper
75g/3oz grated cheese

Pre-heat the oven to Gas 4/180C

Slice the marrow in half, lengthways; scoop out the seeds and discard. Place the marrow halves, side by side, on a baking tray.

Heat the oil and gently fry the spring onion greens and chilli until soft. Add the mince and cook for 2-3 minutes, stirring to break up the meat.

Stir in the passata, lamb stock, spices, and sultanas (if using). Bring to the boil, stir and reduce the heat and simmer gently for 15 minutes. Season and remove from the heat to cool slightly before spooning the meat filling evenly into the marrow.

Bake for 25-30 minutes. Top with the grated cheese and return to the oven for another 10 minutes.

If the marrow is fresh, it should not need peeling and will hold its shape better.

Herb Crusted Lamb Steaks

Ingredients   Serves 4

4 lamb steaks
3 tbsp rosemary or mint jelly
150g / 5oz fresh gluten-free bread crumbs
2 tbsp olive oil
2 tbsp garlic infused oil
1 tsp Dijon mustard
40g/1 ½oz melted butter
3 tbsp chopped chives
2 tbsp chopped fresh parsley
Sprig of rosemary, chopped (discard stalk)
Salt and pepper

Preheated the oven to Gas 2/150C

Coat the steaks in the rosemary or mint jelly and set aside to marinade for 30 minutes.

Blend together the breadcrumbs, mustard, olive oil, butter, seasoning, and herbs to form a paste.

Heat the garlic infused oil in a large frying pan. Sear the steaks on both sides for approximately 2 minutes.

Transfer the steaks to a roasting tin. Spoon the paste onto the top of each of the steaks, pressing down to form a crust.

Cook in the pre-heated oven for 30-40 minutes.

Pork Sausages

Ingredients   Makes 12

500g pork mince
1 tsp salt
1 tsp dried marjoram
1 tsp dried thyme
½ bunch spring onion greens, finely chopped
Ground black pepper to taste

Place half of the pork mince into a large bowl with the other ingredients and mix well.

Add the remaining meat and continue to mix until all the ingredients are evenly combined.

Form the mixture into sausage shapes, approximately 50g each.

The sausages can be cooked immediately, but if you have time, leave them to rest for 30 minutes in the fridge.

If freezing them, place on a tray, not touching (this makes it easier to take out the number of sausages you require rather than a solid block!), leave to freeze, then place in a freezer bag and return to the freezer until you need them.

Making sausages is a messy job but it is much easier to do this with your hands than with a spoon!

Cook on the hob in a frying pan with a splash of oil or on the BBQ for approximately 12 minutes, turning to brown all over.
Take care when turning them; remember there are no skins to hold them together!

Cooking in the oven?
20 minutes at Gas Mark 4/180C

Toad in the Hole

Ingredients   Serves 2

6 homemade pork sausages
3 tbsps vegetable oil

Batter
110g/4oz gluten-free, self-raising flour
142ml/4floz lactose-free milk
Pinch of salt
1 egg
1 tsp gluten-free vegetable suet

Pre-heat the oven to Gas 7/220C.

Place all the batter ingredients in a bowl and beat until smooth.

Heat 2 tablespoons of the oil in a roasting pan in the pre-heated oven. Meanwhile, heat the remaining oil in a frying pan and brown the sausages on all sides.

Transfer the sausages to the roasting tin and pour over the batter. Cook for 30 minutes.

**Gluten free sausages are available in supermarkets and butchers
but check the ingredients for onions and garlic.**

Lovely with onion gravy!

Escalope of Pork

Ingredients   Serves 4

4 pork leg steaks
125g /4oz gluten-free fresh breadcrumbs (approx. 3 slices)
1 egg, beaten
4tbsp gluten-free plain flour
Salt and pepper
2 tsp dried parsley
2 tsp dried thyme
2-3 tbsp oil

Place the breadcrumbs in a bowl and mix in the seasoning and herbs.

One at a time, place the pork steaks on a chopping board, cover with cling film and bash with a rolling pin until the steak is approximately ½ cm thick. Repeat with all steaks.
Coat each steak with flour, then egg and finally coat with an even covering of breadcrumbs.

Heat 2 tbsp of oil in a large frying pan. Place the steaks in the pan and fry for 3 minutes. Turn and fry for another 3 minutes, adding a little more oil if necessary.

Pork Stroganoff

Ingredients   Serves 4

500g pork loin, cut into very thin strips
1 bunch spring onion greens, finely chopped
1 tbsp garlic infused oil
2 tsp paprika
1 tbsp brandy
375ml /14oz lactose-free cream
1 tsp lemon juice
1 tsp dried tarragon
Sprinkle of salt
Ground black pepper to taste

Add the lemon juice to the cream and set aside.

In a large frying pan, heat the oil and fry the spring onion greens until soft. Add the strips of meat and fry for 2-3 minutes, stirring to ensure the meat browns on all sides.

Tip the brandy in, stir and add the soured cream, paprika, tarragon, and seasoning.

Bring to the boil; reduce to a medium heat for 2 minutes to allow the sauce to thicken slightly.

Serve with wild rice.

Freeze the meat for 20mins to ease the cutting.

Beef sirloin can be used instead.

Cheesey Pork Meatballs

Ingredients   Serves 4

500g minced pork
2 tsp thyme
Salt and pepper
240g cheddar cheese cut into 1 ½ cm cubes (lactose-free cheese, if preferred)

Sauce
1 tin chopped tomatoes
1 bunch spring onion greens, chopped
2 red peppers, sliced
1 green pepper, sliced
1 large fresh chilli, finely chopped (deseeded if required)
1 Knorr ham stock cube
Splash of white wine
1 bay leaf
Salt and pepper
1 tblsp garlic infused oil
1 tblsp vegetable oil

Place the pork mince in a large bowl and add the thyme and seasoning. Stir well to combine the ingredients. Divide the meat into small balls (about the size of a golf ball). Push a cube of cheese into each ball, making sure the cheese is completely covered.

Heat the oil in a large pan and fry the spring onion greens and chilli for 1 minute, add the meatballs and continue frying for 6-8 minutes, stirring to turn and brown the meatballs evenly.

Add the peppers and splash in the white wine; fry for a further 2 minutes. Pour in the tomatoes, adding the bay leaf and stock cube to the mix. Season to taste.

Simmer gently for 20 – 30 minutes, until the meatballs are cooked through.

Chicken & Vegetable Pie

Ingredients   Serves 4 - 6

225g /8oz short crust gluten-free pastry
225g /8oz rough puff pastry
2 chicken breasts, diced
150g /5oz frozen diced mixed vegetables
1 tbsp vegetable oil
200ml /10floz chicken stock
3 tbsp thickening granules (or 2 tbsp cornflour mixed with 2 tbsp water)
A few drops of gravy browning
½ tsp mixed herbs
Salt and pepper

Pre-heat the oven to Gas Mark 7/220C.

Line a 20cm /8in pie dish with the pastry. Line the pastry with foil or baking parchment, fill the case with baking beans, dried pulses, or rice to prevent the bottom from rising.

Bake for 10 minutes.

Heat the oil and fry the chicken until lightly browned. Add the mixed vegetables, stir for 1 minute. Pour in the stock and add the thickening granules whilst stirring; bring to the boil and reduce the heat. Simmer for 10 minutes, stirring occasionally.

Stir in the mixed herbs, the gravy browning, and seasoning. The sauce should be a smooth, thick gravy.

Pour the mixture into to the pastry case and cover with the rough puff pastry.

Reduce the oven temperature to Gas Mark 5/190C and bake for 30 minutes. Cover with foil and cook for a further 20-30 minutes until the top is golden and crisp.

As an alternative to lining the pastry, prick the bottom all over and paint with a little beaten egg.

Chicken & Ham Crumble-topped Pie

Ingredients   Serves 4 - 6

225g /8oz short crust gluten-free pastry
150g /5oz Savoury crumble mix (see recipe)
1 large chicken breast, diced
1 gammon steak, diced
25g /1oz gluten-free plain flour, seasoned
1 tsp garlic infused oil
1 knob of butter
2 large handful green leek tops
200ml /10floz chicken stock
1 tbsp cream cheese with chives (lactose-free if preferred)
½ tsp mixed herbs

Pre-heat the oven to Gas Mark 7/220C.

Line a 20cm /8in pie dish with the pastry. Line the pastry with foil or baking parchment, fill the case with baking beans, dried pulses or rice to prevent the bottom from rising.

Bake for 15 minutes.

Coat the chicken and gammon with the seasoned flour. Heat the oil and butter, fry the chicken and gammon until lightly browned. Add the green leek tops, stir for 1 minute. Pour in the stock, stirring, bring to the boil, and reduce the heat. Simmer for 10 minutes, stirring occasionally

Stir in the mixed herbs and the cream cheese. The sauce should be a smooth creamy consistency.

Pour the mixture into to the pastry case and cover with the crumble mix.

Reduce the oven temperature to Gas Mark 4/180C and bake for 30-40 minutes or until the crumble is golden and crisp.

Add more stock if needed, or thicken with some thickening granules.

BBQ Chicken

Ingredients   Serves 4

8 large or 12 small boneless chicken thighs
2 tsps garlic infused oil
1 tbsp olive oil
1 bunch spring onion greens, chopped
2 tsps fresh thyme, chopped
300ml /10floz tomato sauce
2 tbsps muscovado sugar
50ml /2floz red/white wine vinegar
½ tsp dry mustard
1 tsp ground cumin
1 tsp paprika or smoked paprika
Salt and pepper

Pre-heat the oven to Gas 5/190C.

Heat the oils. In batches, brown the chicken thighs all over. Remove using a slotted spoon and place in a roasting tin. Place the spring onion greens into the frying pan and fry until soft. Add the remaining ingredients, stir, and bring to the boil.

Carefully pour the sauce over the chicken pieces.

Cook in the oven for 40-50 minutes.

Alternatively…
Place in a slow cooker on low heat for 6-8 hours for a meal ready for when you come home!

Don't forget to check the tomato sauce ingredients for onions/garlic.

Kicking Southern Fried Chicken

Ingredients   Serves 4

500g chicken mini fillets
1 large egg
2 tbsp garlic infused oil
Gluten free plain flour, to coat chicken

<u>Breadcrumb mix</u>
150g/5oz fresh gluten-free breadcrumbs
2 tsps cayenne pepper
½ tsp paprika
1 tsp dried thyme
1 tsp dried oregano
¼ tsp salt
½ tsp ground black pepper

Pre-heat the oven to Gas 6/200C.

Brush the chicken mini fillets, all over, with garlic infused oil and set aside for 20-30 minutes.

Mix the breadcrumbs with the herbs, salt, and pepper. Rub through thoroughly to ensure an even mix.

Coat the chicken with the flour. Break the eggs into a bowl and beat. Dip each fillet in the beaten egg and then into the breadcrumbs. Lightly spray each fillet, both sides, with vegetable oil.

Place the fillets on a lightly oiled baking tray. Bake for 20 minutes on the top shelf; turn and bake for 10 -15 minutes on the middle shelf.

Pour about 6 tablespoons flour (add more if needed) and the breadcrumb mix into separate bags. Put one fillet at a time in and shake.

This helps to avoid messy hands!

Coat all the pieces with flour, then work with one piece to egg and breadcrumb before moving to the next piece.

Coq Au Vin

Ingredients   Serves 4

8 Chicken thighs (600-700g /1½ lb)
125g /4oz bacon, chopped
1 bunch spring onion greens, chopped
1 large carrot, finely grated
1 tsp garlic infused oil
1 tbsp vegetable oil
½ tsp asafoetida
450ml red wine
2 tsp soft brown sugar
1 bouquet garni
Pinch of ground nutmeg
1 tbsp tomato puree
I Knorr ham stock cube
Salt and pepper

Heat the oil in a large, flameproof casserole. Brown the chicken thighs and remove to a plate. Add the bacon, spring onion greens, and asafoetida to the oil and fry until the bacon is cooked.

Stir in the grated carrot and cook for a few minutes then add the flour. Stir until it forms a paste. Gradually add the wine, stirring continuously. Add the remaining ingredients and mix well.

Carefully place the chicken thighs into the casserole and bring to a steady simmer. Cook on the hob or in the oven (Gas 4/180C) for 45 minutes -1 hour, until the chicken is cooked through.

It may be easier to brown the chicken in several batches.

 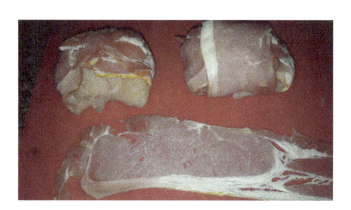

Stuffed Chicken Wrapped in Bacon

Ingredients   Serves 4

4 chicken breasts
125g /4oz cheddar cheese, cut into 4 equal pieces
8 rashers back bacon
Garlic infused oil

Pre-heat the oven to Gas Mark 7/220C.

Taking one breast at a time, place it on a chopping board and cover with a piece of cling film. Using a rolling pin, beat the chicken breast flat. Repeat with the remaining breasts.

Lightly brush the upper surface of the chicken with garlic infused oil. Place a piece of cheese in the centre of each breast and wrap the chicken around it.

Place one rasher of bacon on the board and, using the back of a knife, carefully run the blade along the rasher, like spreading butter. This will stretch the rasher. Repeat with all the bacon rashers. Using 2 rashers of bacon for each chicken breast, wrap the stuffed chicken.

Roll each chicken breast tightly in cling film, twisting the ends, to hold the chicken in shape. Place in the fridge for at least 30 minutes.

Remove from the fridge and carefully unwrap the breasts; removing the cling film.

Heat a little more garlic infused oil in a frying pan and sear the breasts, browning the chicken roll all over.

Place in a roasting tin and bake in the oven for 15-20 minutes or until the chicken in cooked through.

You can hit the chicken quite hard but take care not to tear the flesh.

Alternatively the chicken can be left in the cling film and steamed for 20 minutes then, with the cling film removed, browned in the frying pan.

Hunters Chicken

Ingredients Serves 4

4 chicken breasts
125g /4oz cheese, grated

BBQ Sauce
1 tbsp garlic infused oil
1 bunch spring onion greens, chopped
2 tsps fresh thyme, chopped
300ml /10floz tomato sauce
2 tbsps muscovado sugar
50ml /2floz red/white wine vinegar
½ tsp dry mustard
1 tsp ground cumin
1 tsp paprika or smoked paprika
Salt and pepper

Pre-heat the oven to Gas Mark 6/200C.

Heat the oil in a pan and fry the spring onion greens until soft. Add the remaining ingredients and stir well. Bring to the boil, lower the heat and simmer for 20 minutes.

Place the chicken breasts in a roasting tin, cover with foil and cook for 15 minutes in the oven.

Remove the chicken from the oven and pour the BBQ sauce over the breasts. Sprinkle the cheese on top. Return to the oven and cook for a further 10 minutes.

Bacon & Cheese Croquettas

Ingredients   Serves 4

<u>Filling</u>
1 tbsp garlic infused oil
½ bunch spring onion greens, finely chopped
300g /10oz smoked bacon, finely chopped
100g /4oz Cheddar cheese (or lactose-free cheese), grated
60 g /2 ½oz gluten-free plain flour
75ml /3oz ham/chicken stock
325ml /10floz lactose-free milk
Pinch nutmeg
Salt and pepper

<u>Coating</u>
75g /3oz gluten-free plain flour
1 large egg, beaten egg
100g /4oz gluten-free dried breadcrumbs

Vegetable oil for deep frying.

Heat the oil in a saucepan and fry the spring onion greens and bacon for 2 minutes.

Stir in the flour and mix well. Continue stirring whilst gradually pouring in the milk. Stir until the sauce begins to thicken. Add the cheese, nutmeg, and seasoning. Continue to stir until the sauce is very thick.

The mixture will be thick enough when you push a spoon across the bottom of the pan and it divides the mix, showing the pan.

Remove from the heat and place the mixture in a shallow baking tray; leave to cool. Once cool enough, place in the fridge for approximately 30 minutes.

The mixture is ready when you can cut it into chunks. Divide the mixture into walnut sized balls. Coat each ball with the flour, dip into the beaten egg and coat evenly, and finally, coat with breadcrumbs.

Heat the vegetable oil in a deep fat fryer and carefully place a few croquettas at a time into the basket, fry until golden. Remove and keep warm. Repeat until all croquettas are cooked.

Approximately 4 slices of gluten free bread makes 100g dried breadcrumbs.
Place on a baking sheet and leave in a low oven until crisp.

Fish Pie

Ingredients   Serves 4

25g /1oz butter
25g /1oz gluten free plain flour
1 bunch spring onion greens, chopped
350ml /12floz lactose-free milk
1 pack fish pie mix (approx. 320-400g)
1 tsp Dijon mustard
1 tbsp chopped chives
2 tbsp sweetcorn
2 tbsp frozen peas
75g /3oz grated cheddar cheese or lactose-free cheese
 (Add an additional 40g /1 ½oz grated cheese for topping)
Handful of gluten free breadcrumbs
Salt and pepper

4 large potatoes, cooked and mashed with a knob of butter.

Pre-heat the oven to Gas Mark 5/190C.

Melt the butter in a saucepan and stir-fry the spring onion greens until soft. Stir in the flour and cook for 1-2 minutes. Gradually add the milk, stirring constantly. Add the cheese. Bring to the boil, lower the heat and simmer for 3-4 minutes to thicken. Remove from heat.

Stir the chives, fish, mustard, and vegetables into the sauce; mix well. Pour into a pie dish.

Top with the mashed potato and sprinkle with the breadcrumbs and grated cheese.

Bake in the oven for 20 25 minutes, until the potato is golden.

Salmon Fishcakes

Ingredients   Makes 6

2 salmon fillets, approximately 300g
300g /10oz potato, peeled and diced
1 tbsp tomato sauce
½ tsp dried parsley
½ tsp dried dill
½ tsp dried chilli flakes
1 tsp lemon juice
Salt and pepper

Coating
75g /3oz fresh gluten-free breadcrumbs
1 egg
50g /2oz gluten-free plain flour

Garlic infused oil, for cooking

Boil the potatoes until tender. Leave to cool and mash.

Meanwhile grill the salmon for 4-5 minutes, until they are just cooked. Cool slightly and then break into large flakes, sprinkle with the lemon juice.

Mix the tomato sauce, herbs and seasoning with the mashed potato. Add the salmon and gently fold into the potato mixture.

Divide the mixture into 6 and form into patties. Carefully coat with flour; dip them, one at a time into the egg and then coat evenly with the breadcrumbs.

Place on a tray and chill for 1 hour.

Heat the oil in a frying pan. Add the fishcakes and fry gently for 4-5 minutes each side, or until they are golden brown.

Serve with sweet chilli sauce (see recipe) and salad.

Indian Feasts

Biryani

This recipe can be used in the traditional way to make a Biryani or cooked separately to make a 'wet' sauce and serve the rice separately.

Spice mix

24 whole cloves
2 tsp whole black peppercorn
2 tsp whole cardamom seeds
4 tsp whole cumin seeds
4 tsp ground cinnamon
¾ tsp ground nutmeg

Ingredients   Serves 6

2 tsp garlic infused oil
2 tsp vegetable oil
2 bay leaves
1 bunch spring onions greens finely chopped
2 tsp finely chopped/grated fresh ginger
1 large fresh chilli, finely chopped (keep the seeds in for a hotter spice)
1 tsp asafoetida
1 tsp salt
4 tsp spice mix (see recipe above)
1 tbsp dried coriander leaf
500g lamb, beef or chicken, diced
1 tin chopped tomatoes
200ml stock
125ml lactose-free yogurt
A handful of sultanas (optional)
1tsp garam masala
225g/8oz rice
3 tsp butter

Make stock with 1 stock cube (check ingredients for onion/garlic) or 2tsp Bovril,
or use homemade fresh stock to match the meat

Homemade yoghurt, using lactose free milk, is preferable, but
lactose free cream is a good substitute.

Creamed coconut can also be used but will add a coconut flavour to the sauce.

Heat oils in a heavy bottomed saucepan and add bay leaves; fry until they start to brown. Add ginger, chilli and spring onion greens.

While they fry, mix a little water with the spice mix, asafoetida and salt to make a paste then stir into the saucepan mix and fry for 2 minutes.

Add the meat and stir well to coat with the spices.

When the meat has browned all over, add the tinned tomatoes, stock and coriander leaf. Stir well. Bring to a simmer and reduce heat to low; simmer for 30 minutes.

Meanwhile, rinse the rice until the water runs clear. Leave to drain.

Return to the saucepan and stir in the yoghurt/cream gradually. *Pour the rice onto the curry sauce. Pile it up like a mountain and make a hole in the centre. Dot the rice with butter. Sprinkle on the sultanas.

Cover the casserole dish with foil and put the lid on. Leave on a very low heat for 45-50 minutes.

Check the rice is cooked to your liking, stir to mix adding in the garam masala.

Serve with homemade naan bread (see recipe)

*At this point…If you are making a 'wet' sauce to serve separately with boiled basmati rice, add the sultanas (if using) and place the lid on tightly, leave on a low heat to simmer for 30 minutes.

Vegetable Curry

Ingredients

3 small potatoes, diced
2 carrots, sliced
1 large parsnip, diced
1 small swede, diced
1 bunch spring onion greens, chopped
1 tsp lazy ginger (1 inch fresh ginger)
1 tsp garlic infused oil
1 large chilli
1 aubergine, diced
1 courgette, sliced

4 tbsp vegetable oil
1 tsp fennel seeds
1 tsp whole cumin seeds
1 tbsp ground coriander seeds
½ tsp turmeric
1 tbsp dried coriander leaf
400g passata
½ tsp garam masala

Blend the garlic infused oil with the ginger and chilli to make a paste.

Place the potatoes and root vegetables into a pan and par-boil for 10 minutes. Drain and set aside.

Meanwhile heat the vegetable oil in a large frying pan, add the aubergine and courgette, and cook until they have browned. Remove from the oil with a slotted spoon and set aside on some kitchen paper to drain.

Add the fennel and cumin seeds to the frying pan and fry for 30 seconds. Add the spring onion greens and fry until soft. Stir in the ginger and chilli paste, turmeric, coriander seeds and coriander leaf. Add the passata. Stir to combine. Place all the vegetables in the frying pan and simmer on a low heat until the vegetables are just cooked.

Stir in the garam masala. Continue to stir and cook for a few more minutes until the edges of the vegetables soften and thicken the sauce.

This makes a great main meal or side dish.

Try it with Chicken Biryani.

Bombay Style Potatoes

Ingredients

1 large potato
2 sweet potatoes
1 tbsp chives, chopped
1 small fresh chilli, deseeded and finely chopped
1 tsp asafoetida
1 tsp turmeric
½ tsp ground coriander
½ tsp cumin
5 cardamom pods
2 ½cm/1in cinnamon stick
3 cloves
1 tbsp garlic infused oil
1 tin of chopped tomatoes
1 tbsp tomato puree
Salt and pepper

Peel and dice the potatoes. Par boil for 10 minutes, drain, leaving them in the strainer until needed.

Heat the oil in a large frying pan. Add the whole spices and stir for a few seconds. Lower the heat a little and stir in the chives, chilli and ground spices.

Add the remaining ingredients. Bring to the boil then lower to simmer gently.

Cook for about 20-30 minutes, until the potatoes are soft.

If you like it hot, use more chilli or leave the seeds in and cook as the recipe states. You can also add some cayenne pepper or dried chillies (a little bit at a time!) once you have tasted the sauce!

Cucumber and Mint Yoghurt

Ingredients

275ml/10floz lactose-free yoghurt (see recipe)
¼ of a cucumber
2 tbsp fresh mint, finely chopped
½ tsp ground cumin
¼ tsp cayenne pepper
Salt and pepper

Peel and deseed the cucumber then coarsely grate the flesh. Wrap in kitchen paper or a tea towel and gently squeeze out some of the water.

Beat the yoghurt until smooth and creamy. Stir in all the other ingredients and place in the fridge until required.

Tandoori Chicken

Ingredients   Serves 4-6

500g Chicken breasts
1 tsp each yellow and red food colouring
1 tsp garlic infused oil
1 tbsp vegetable oil

Marinade
½ tsp salt
½ tsp garam masala
¼ tsp cayenne pepper
½ tsp asefoetida
1.5cm/½in cube fresh ginger, grated
2 tbsp lemon juice

Slice each of the chicken breasts into 6-8 pieces and place in a bowl. Pour on the food colouring and stir to coat the chicken all over.

Mix the marinade ingredients together and pour over the coloured chicken pieces. Stir well. Cover and set aside in the fridge for at least 2 hours, preferably overnight.

Drain the marinade from the chicken and discard.

Heat the oils in a large frying pan on a medium heat and gently fry the chicken, turning frequently until cooked through.

Try diced lamb as an alternative to chicken.

Serve hot or cold with rice or salad.

Alternatively use Tikka Masala sauce (see recipe).

You can also put the chicken pieces onto kebab skewers and cook over a BBQ. Add chunks of red pepper between the chicken for added taste.

Chicken Tikka Masala

Ingredients   Serves 4-6

500g tandoori Chicken, freshly cooked

Masala sauce

4 tbsp tomato puree
1 in cube of fresh ginger, very finely grated
250ml/8floz lactose-free cream
1 tsp garam masala
½ tsp salt
¼ tsp sugar
1 fresh chilli, very finely chopped (seeds removed – optional)
1 tbsp fresh coriander leaf, finely chopped
4 tsp lemon juice
1 tsp ground cumin
110g/40z unsalted butter
50g creamed coconut

Making the sauce

Put the tomato puree into a measuring jug and add water to make 250ml/8floz. Add all the ingredients **except** the butter and creamed coconut, stir to mix.

Melt the butter in a heavy bottomed pan. Add the creamed coconut and stir to melt. Stir in the mixture from the jug.

Bring to a gentle simmer and stir for 1 minute.

Add the Tandoori chicken pieces to the sauce; stir through and serve with Basmati rice.

Alternatively, pour the sauce into a serving jug as an accompaniment; serving the tandoori chicken pieces separately.

Try this sauce with tandoori lamb for a change!

If you can't tolerate butter, use Ghee (clarified butter).

For a lower fat version, Clover light works well!

Seekh Kebab

Ingredients   Serves 4-6

500g minced lamb
½ tsp salt
½ tsp ground pepper
2 tbsp fresh coriander, finely chopped
2 tbsp fresh mint, finely chopped
1 tsp ground cumin
1/2tsp ground coriander
1 tsp garam masala
5 tsp paprika
1 tbsp garlic infused oil
2 tbsp natural lactose-free yoghurt
1 fresh chilli (de-seeded if preferred), finely chopped

12 wooden skewers

Place the skewers in a baking tray and cover with water. Leave to soak for at least 30 minutes (this helps to stop the skewers from burning on the BBQ or grill).

Place all the ingredients in the bowl of a food processor. Blend until they are well mixed.

Divide the mixture into 12 balls. Take a skewer and mould the 'ball' of meat mixture around it to form a sausage shape. Repeat with remaining skewers.

Place in the fridge to rest for 30 minutes.

Cook under a hot grill or on the BBQ, turning carefully, until cooked through.

Naan Bread

Ingredients   Makes 4

200g/8oz gluten-free bread flour and a little extra for dusting when kneading
1 tsp dried yeast
1½ tsp sugar
75ml/3floz hand-hot, lactose-free milk
¼ tsp salt
½ tsp baking powder
½ egg, beaten
1 tbsp vegetable oil
2 tbsp lactose-free natural yoghurt

Pre-heated the oven to Gas 8/230C

Sieve together the flour, baking powder and salt. Stir in the sugar and yeast. Make a well in the flour mix and pour in the oil, yoghurt, and egg. Mix to a soft dough. Cover loosely with cling film and place in a warm place to rise for about an hour.

Dust the surface of a pastry board or worktop with gluten free flour and turn the dough out of the bowl and knead for 1 minute.

Divide the dough into 4 and, working quickly, place on a hot baking sheet or hot pizza stone and spread out to teardrop shapes.

Place in the oven for 4-5 minutes. Remove, sprinkle with water and brown under a hot grill.

To make a garlic and coriander naan, simply replace 1 tsp of oil with garlic infused oil and add 1tbsp fresh coriander, finely chopped.

These freeze really well. Remove from the oven and cool before freezing. To re-heat, thaw, sprinkle with water and grill to brown, or place in a hot oven from frozen for 5 minutes.

These naan will not be as soft as traditional naan. They tend to have a crisp outside but are a good substitute.

Rogan Josh

Ingredients   Serves 4-6

500g diced lamb or chicken
1 tbsp garlic infused oil
1 tbsp vegetable oil
2 fresh chillies, de-seeded (optional) and finely chopped
1 bunch spring onion greens, chopped
8 whole cardamom pods
1 bay leaf
6 whole cloves
5 whole peppercorns
2cm /¾ in cinnamon stick
1 tbsp fennel seeds
½ tsp asafoetida
1 tsp paprika
1½ tsp dried ginger powder
1 tsp ground coriander seeds
2 tsp ground cumin seeds
1 tsp salt
3 tbsp lactose-free natural yogurt
1 tin chopped tomatoes
2 peppers (red and/or green), diced
½ tsp garam masala
1 tbsp fresh coriander leaf, chopped

Heat the oils and add the whole spices; fry for 30 seconds. Add the meat, chillies, and salt; stir for 5 minutes. Stir in the ground spices and the tinned tomatoes. Fill the tomato tin with water and pour into the pan. Stir well and bring to a boil. Slowly add the yogurt, stirring, bring back to boiling point.

Lower the heat and cover with a lid; simmer for 30 minutes for chicken/1hour for lamb or until cooked through and tender.

Add the peppers, cover, and cook for a further 45 minutes.

Stir in the garam masala and coriander leaf and serve.

For an extra special dish, use tandoori chicken or lamb.

Chicken Korma

Ingredients   Serves 4

4 chicken breasts, diced
2 ½cm/1in cube fresh ginger
4 tbsp garlic infused oil
10 whole cardamom pods
1in stick of cinnamon
2 bay leaves
5 whole cloves
1 bunch spring onion greens, chopped
1 fresh chilli (deseeded for milder spice)
2 tsp cumin
1 tsp turmeric
7 tbsp lactose-free natural yoghurt
200g creamed coconut
250ml lactose-free cream
1 tsp salt
1 tsp garam masala
1 tbsp sultanas and/or almonds (optional)
2 tbsp toasted desiccated coconut

Blend the ginger and chilli with 4 tbsp of water to create a smooth paste.

Heat the oil in a large casserole pot, add the chicken pieces, and stir until the meat is lightly browned on all sides. Remove with a slotted spoon and set aside.

Put the whole spices into the hot oil and stir for a few seconds. Add the ginger and chilli paste and spring onion greens to the pot and continue stirring for 3-4 minutes.

Add the cumin and turmeric and cook, stirring constantly, until the oil begins to separate. Pour in the yoghurt gradually and stir until all the yoghurt has combined.

Return the chicken to the pot, along with the cream, creamed coconut and salt. Lower the heat to a gentle simmer and cook for 20 minutes.

Remove from the heat and stir in the garam masala. Sprinkle the toasted coconut, sultanas, and/or almonds (if using) over the top and serve.

Mediterranean Feasts

Fresh Gluten - Free Pasta

Ingredients   Serves 4

200g/7oz gluten free bread flour
2tsp xanthan gum
½ tsp salt
3 medium sized eggs, beaten

Sift the flour with the xanthan gum and stir in the salt. Add the eggs and mix with a fork until the mixture begins to cling together.

Turn the contents out of the bowl onto a floured surface and, using your hands, bring the mixture together to form a ball of dough.

Knead until smooth. Place in a plastic bag and put in the fridge to rest for 30 minutes.

If you have a pasta machine, work the dough through the rollers to the finest thickness. Alternatively place the dough between 2 sheets of cling film and roll out with a rolling pin to approximately 2mm.

Use raw when layering a lasagne or bring a large saucepan of water to the boil, add a splash of olive oil and gently stir in the pasta. Reduce the heat to medium and continue to boil for 3-4 minutes. Drain and serve with parmesan cheese or your favourite sauce.

Spinach Pasta

255g/9oz gluten free bread flour
1 tsp xanthan gum
¼ tsp salt
2 eggs
1tbsp olive oil
85g/3½oz spinach puree

Use the method as above, adding the spinach with the eggs.

Use the dough flat for lasagne or pass through the pasta machine cutters/slice with a sharp knife and steady hand for tagliattelle or spaghetti.

Lamb & Mint Ravioli

Ingredients   Serves 4

150g fresh gluten free pasta
1 tsp vegetable oil

Filling

150g cooked minced lamb
1 tsp garlic infused oil
1 tbsp spring onion greens, finely chopped (from sauce ingredients)
4 tsp fresh mint leaves, finely chopped
4 tsp grated hard Italian cheese i.e parmesan

Sauce

1 bunch spring onion greens, chopped
2 tsp fresh rosemary, chopped
1 carrot, finely diced
1 tbsp garlic infused oil
500g passata
200ml/7floz red wine
400ml/14floz lamb stock
1 tbsp tomato puree
Salt and pepper

If you have a pasta machine, work the dough through the rollers to the finest thickness. Alternatively place the dough between 2 sheets of cling film and roll out with a rolling pin to approximately 2mm. Using a 7.5cm/3in pastry cutter, cut out circles of pasta, rerolling the leftovers until all the pasta has been cut into circles. Cover with a damp tea towel.

Filling

Heat the garlic infused oil in a saucepan and stir-fry the spring onion greens until soft. Add the remaining ingredients and mix well.

Lay the pasta circles out into 2 equal rows. Place a teaspoonful of the lamb mixture onto the centre of one circle, lightly moisten the edge, and place another circle on top. Gently press all around the edge. Repeat until all the circles have been used. Re-cover with the tea towel whilst you make the sauce or cover with cling film and place in the fridge for later.

Sauce

Using the same saucepan as for the filling, pour in the garlic infused oil and heat. Stir-fry the spring onion greens, rosemary, and carrot until soft.

Add the red wine and stir for 1 minute. Pour in the passata, lamb stock and tomato puree, and seasoning. Stir well and bring to the boil. Reduce the heat and simmer for 30 minutes.

When the sauce is cooked, bring a large pan of water to the boil. Pour in the teaspoonful of vegetable oil and stir. Add the ravioli carefully, gently stirring to ensure they don't stick together. Simmer for 3-4 minutes. Drain and place in a serving dish or individual plates. Dress with the sauce. Serve immediately.

Spaghetti Bolognaise

Ingredients   Serves 4

500g mince beef
1 tsp garlic infused oil
1 bunch of spring onions greens, chopped
1 tsp Bovril
1tsp dried oregano
½ tsp dried basil
1 carton/tin chopped tomatoes
1 tblsp tomato puree
splash of red wine
salt and pepper

Gluten free spaghetti

Heat oil and fry mince and spring onion greens until the meat has browned, stirring to break up the mince. Add remaining ingredients and cook for approximately 30 minutes on a slow simmer. Stir occasionally to ensure that it isn't catching on the bottom of the pan.

Cook pasta and serve.

Dried gluten free pasta may take a little longer to cook than normal pasta.

Alternatively…try making your own pasta (see recipe).

Tuna & Tomato Sauce

Ingredients   Serves 4

360g/3 tins tuna chunks
200g fresh gluten free pasta dough (see recipe) or 300g dried gluten free pasta
Grated parmesan cheese
Sauce
2 tbsp garlic infused oil
½ bunch spring onion greens, finely chopped
2 cans chopped tomatoes
2 tbsp tomato puree
2 tbsp fresh basil, chopped
1 tsp sugar
Salt and pepper

Drain the tuna and set aside.

Heat the oil in a sauce pan and stir-fry the spring onion greens until soft.

Carefully pour in the chopped tomatoes (they may spit a little). Stir in the tomato puree, basil, and sugar. Season to taste.

Bring the pan to the boil, lower the heat, and simmer for 40 minutes, stirring occasionally.

Meanwhile cook the pasta as directed in the recipe or on the packet.

Add the tuna and stir into the sauce, being careful not to break up the tuna chunks. Heat until the tuna has warmed through.

Drain the pasta and divide into 4 bowls. Pour the tuna and tomato sauce over the pasta. Serve immediately, with grated parmesan cheese.

Arrabiata Sauce

Ingredients   Serves 4

1 tin chopped tomatoes
500ml passata
2 tbsp fresh basil, chopped
1 fresh chilli (deseeded – optional)
2 tbsp garlic infused oil
Salt and pepper

Heat the garlic infused oil in a pan, add the chilli, and stir. Carefully pour in the tomatoes and passata, beware this may spit a little. Add the basil and seasoning.

Bring to the boil, lower the heat and simmer gently for 30 minutes.

Serve with your favourite pasta

Carbonara with Chicken & Bacon

Ingredients　　Serves 2-3

2tbsp garlic infused oil
2 chicken breasts, cut into strips
8 rashers smoked bacon, chopped
250ml /9floz lactose-free cream
Handful fresh basil, finely chopped
200g /7oz cheddar cheese, grated
Salt and pepper

250g/1lb pasta (eg spaghetti, tagliatelle , or fusilli)

Cook the pasta to al dente.

Whilst the pasta is cooking, heat the garlic infused oil in a pan. Fry the chicken and bacon until cooked, stirring to stop the bacon clumping together.

Pour in the cream and warm over a gentle heat. Add the drained pasta, cheese, and seasoning. Stir until thick and creamy.

Just before serving, stir through the fresh basil.

This has lots of cheese so you may prefer to use lactose-free cheddar.

Italian Meatballs

Ingredients   Serves 4

Meatballs

500g/1 lb minced beef
1 tsp Bovril
1 tbsp each of basil, oregano and chives, chopped
1 tbsp spring onion greens, chopped
½ fresh chilli, deseeded and finely chopped
Drizzle garlic infused oil
Salt and pepper

Sauce

500ml passata
½ tsp fresh basil, chopped
½ tsp fresh oregano, chopped
1 tsp Bovril
2 tsp brown sugar
50ml/2 floz red wine
1 tsp garlic infused oil
50ml 2 floz lactose-free cream

Accompaniment

1 tbsp garlic infused oil
300g fresh gluten-free tagliatelle
Parsley for garnish

Place the mince in a bowl and thoroughly mix with the other ingredients. Form into small meatballs (cherry tomato size). Heat the oil in a frying pan and add the meatballs. Cook until browned all over (gently shaking the pan regularly will make the balls turn and prevent sticking). Remove and set aside on a plate with kitchen paper.

Place all the sauce ingredients into a saucepan and bring to the boil. Reduce heat and add the meatballs. Simmer for 20 minutes, until meatballs are cooked through and the sauce has reduced slightly.

Meanwhile, boil a large pan of salted water and cook the pasta.

Place the pasta in a large dish and pour over the sauce. Garnish with some chopped parsley.

Chicken Risotto

Ingredients   Serves 4

300g/10oz Arborio rice
1 tsp garlic infused oil
1 tbsp vegetable oil
1 green pepper, diced
1 small red pepper, diced
1 cup sweet corn
4 rashers of smoked bacon, chopped
3 large chicken thighs, diced
1 bunch spring onion greens, chopped
1 tsp fresh basil, finely chopped
1 tsp fresh thyme, finely chopped
60ml/2 ½floz white wine
1 ltr /1 ¾pt homemade chicken stock
Salt and pepper

Heat the oils in a large, deep sided frying pan or heavy bottomed saucepan. Add the spring onion greens, bacon, and chicken and fry for about 5 minutes. Stir in half of the peppers, the sweet corn, and the rice, and continue frying for another few minutes.

Pour in the wine, stir and then add about 1/3 of the stock. Bring the pan to a simmer. When the stock has been absorbed add another 1/3, stir. When this has absorbed, add the remaining stock and peppers and stir through.

Sprinkle the herbs over the top.

When the rice is cooked, check seasoning, stir and serve.

You can substitute the homemade chicken stock with stock made from a stock cube, but check the ingredients for gluten, onions and garlic.

Lasagne

Ingredients   Serves 4- 6

Meat sauce
Use recipe for spaghetti bolognaise

Cheese sauce

725ml/1¼pt lactose-free milk
75g/3oz margarine
75g/3oz gluten-free plain flour
225g/8oz cheddar cheese or lactose-free cheese, grated (save a little to sprinkle on the top)
1tsp dried English mustard
Salt and pepper

Approximately 8-9 gluten-free lasagne sheets (pre-cooking if required)

Make the meat sauce as per the instruction for spaghetti bolognaise.

Pre-heat the oven to Gas 5/190C.

While the meat sauce is simmering, make the cheese sauce.

Sift the mustard into the flour and mix. Melt the margarine in a saucepan and stir in the flour and mustard. Keep over the heat and stir to form a smooth paste. Add the milk slowly, stirring constantly until the sauce begins to boil. Add the cheese and continue stirring until it comes back to a boil. Simmer and stir for 2 minutes. The sauce should now be smooth and creamy.

When both the sauces are ready, begin making the layers. Cover the bottom of a deep baking dish (approximately 26cmx20cm/10in x in) with about one third of the meat sauce. Pour a little of the cheese sauce over the meat sauce and cover with sheets of lasagne. Repeat this, finishing with a thick layer of cheese sauce on top of the last layer of lasagne. Sprinkle with the reserved grated cheese. Bake in the oven for 40-50 minutes.

If you warm the milk, it will mix in more smoothly to the roux.

Whoops! The sauce is lumpy and whisking it doesn't help? Pour it into a blender and blend until smooth.

Test that the pasta has cooked by inserting a knife into the middle of the dish. If there is no resistance, the lasagne is ready.

Paella

Ingredients   Serves 4

225g/8oz cooked prawns
150g /5oz smoked bacon, diced
2 chicken breasts, diced
1½ tbsp garlic infused oil
1 bunch spring onion greens, chopped
1 tsp paprika (smoked paprika if preferred)
250g /9oz paella rice
700ml /1¼ pints chicken stock
2 peppers (red/yellow), chopped
2 tbsp each of peas and sweetcorn
400g /14oz tin chopped tomatoes
Salt and pepper

Heat 1 tablespoon of the oil and fry the chicken and bacon until browned. Set aside. Pour in the remaining oil; heat and fry the spring onion greens until soft. Add the rice and paprika and stir to mix. Pour in the stock, stirring, bring to the boil, and reduce the heat. Simmer for 10 minutes.

Return the chicken and bacon to the pan and add the prawns, peppers, peas, sweetcorn and tomatoes. Cook for a further 10 minutes or until the rice is tender (adding a little more stock if needed) and the chicken is cooked through. Season to taste.

Pizza Dough

Ingredients   Makes 4 x 18cm /7in pizzas

Pizza base

110g /4oz gluten free plain flour
110g /4oz gluten free bread flour
20ml /4tsp lactose-free milk
1 tbsp sugar
1 tsp baking powder
¾ tsp salt
1 tsp xanthan gum
1 ½ tsp instant dried yeast
225ml /8floz warm water
1 ½ tbsp olive oil

Preheat the oven to Gas 7/220C.

Pour the warm water and olive oil into a small bowl, sprinkle on the yeast. Stir to combine and set aside for approximately 30 minutes, until bubbly.

Place the remaining dry ingredients together into the bowl of an electric mixer (or large bowl and use a hand mixer). Mix to blend.

When the yeast mixture is ready, add to the dry ingredients, and beat on a medium-high speed for 4 minutes. The mixture will be thick and sticky (more like cake mix than bread dough). Cover and leave to rest for 30 minutes.

Lightly oil the bottom of 4, 7/18cm cake tins. Divide the dough between the tins and using a spatula spread the dough across the bottoms.

Bake in the oven for 4 or 5 minutes, until the dough has become opaque and set. Remove from the oven and top with pizza sauce and your favourite toppings.

Return to the oven and bake for 10-15 minutes.

These pizza bases are great for freezing. Wrap separately.

Remove from the freezer and allow to thaw whilst you prepare your toppings and cook as fresh.

Pizza Sauce

Ingredients   Serves 4

500g passata
1 bunch spring onion greens, finely chopped
¼ tsp asafoetida
1 tsp fresh basil and oregano (mixed)
Salt and pepper
2 tsp brown sugar
1 tsp garlic infused oil.

Heat the garlic infused oil in a pan. Fry the spring onion greens to soften, stir in the asafoetida. Add the other ingredients and bring to the boil, stirring continuously. Reduce the heat and simmer gently until the sauce has thickened.

Try combining cheddar and mozzarella or Feta. These are low in lactose.

Add sliced peppers, sweetcorn, chives, ham, homemade tandoori chicken, or minced beef, to suit your taste!

Moussaka

Ingredients   Serves 4

400g/14oz lamb or mutton mince
2 tsp garlic infused oil
1 bunch spring onion greens, chopped
400g/14oz chopped tomatoes
1 small sprig fresh rosemary (1 tsp dried rosemary)
1 tbsp fresh, chopped oregano or 1 tsp dried oregano
Salt and pepper
2 large aubergines, sliced
5 tbsps vegetable oil

Sauce
750ml/25floz lactose-free milk
75g/3oz margarine
75g/3oz gluten-free plain flour
1 egg, beaten
125g/4oz grated cheddar

Pre-heat the oven to Gas 5/190C.

Heat the oil in a saucepan and gently fry the spring onion greens
until soft. Add the mince and stir-fry until all the meat is brown. Pour in the tinned tomatoes and add the herbs and seasoning. Bring to the boil then reduce the heat and simmer for 20-30 minutes.

Meanwhile, fry the aubergine slices for 2-3 minutes each side. Add more oil if necessary.

Cover the bottom of a large ovenproof dish with 1/3 of the aubergines. Top with ½ of the meat sauce. Repeat the layers and place a final layer of aubergines on top.

To make the sauce, melt the butter gently in a saucepan and stir in the flour. Beat the roux until it is smooth. Gradually pour in the milk, stirring continuously with a wooden spoon, allowing all the milk to be incorporated before adding more milk. When about half the milk has been added, use a whisk to ensure a smooth sauce and add the remaining milk in larger amounts. Remove from the heat and allow to cool slightly before whisking in the beaten egg. Season and pour the sauce over the layers of meat and aubergines. Sprinkle the grated cheese evenly over the dish.

Bake in the oven for 45-50 minutes.

For a garlic flavour, substitute 1 tbsp of vegetable oil for garlic infused oil

Some cooks suggest sprinkling the aubergines with salt and leaving for 10 minutes before rinsing and patting dry, then frying. I have tried both methods and tend to go straight to frying.

Greek Feta Salad

Ingredients   Serves 4

450g /1lb fresh tomatoes, cored and chopped into chunks
½ bunch spring onion greens, chopped
6 tbsp olive oil
Juice of 1 lemon
Handful of fresh flat leaf parsley, trim off the stems
Handful of fresh mint, trim off the stems
200g feta cheese, broken into large chunks
20 black olives
Black pepper
Salt

Place all the ingredients together in a large bowl and gently mix, being careful not to break up the feta any more. Season with black pepper and salt, to taste.

Spicy Moroccan Chicken Couscous

Ingredients   Serves 4

250g/9oz maize couscous
Chicken stock (see couscous directions for amount)
3tbsp garlic infused oil
1 bunch spring onion greens, chopped
2 large chicken breasts, sliced
2 tbsp curry paste (see recipe)
175g/6oz tinned mandarins (drained from juice)
20g/1oz fresh coriander, chopped

Prepare the couscous as stated on the pack, using chicken stock instead of water.

Heat the oil in a deep frying pan and fry the spring onion greens until soft. Add the chicken slices and stir-fry until the meat is seared on all sides.

Stir in the curry paste and cook until the chicken is tender and cooked through, stirring occasionally.

Add the couscous, mandarins, and coriander. Toss until hot.

Serve with plain yoghurt.

Lamb Tajine

Ingredients Serves 4-6

600g/1¼lb lamb, diced
1 large bunch spring onion greens, chopped
1 tbsp garlic infused oil
2 tbsp vegetable oil
3 tbsp gluten-free plain flour
1 tbsp cinnamon
1 tbsp ground cumin
½ tsp turmeric
1 tsp salt
Pepper
500g passata
10floz/300ml homemade lamb stock or 1 stock cube with 10floz/300ml water
2 tbsp brown sugar
3 tbsp sulatans or tinned mandarins
Fresh parsley and coriander leaves, chopped

Pre-heat the oven to Gas 2/150C.

Heat the oil in a heavy oven-proof casserole dish on the hob. Add the coated lamb, in small batches, removing each batch when the meat has browned, to a plate. When all the lamb has been lightly fried, add the spring onion greens to the pan and fry until they soften.

Return all the meat to the pan and add the passata, stock, sugar, and fruit. Stir well and bring to the boil. Cover and place in the oven for 2 hours or until the meat is tender.

Serve with chopped herbs sprinkled on top.

**Mix the flour, cinnamon, cumin, turmeric, and seasoning together in a plastic bag.
Add the diced lamb; shake and coat the lamb with the flour mix.**

Feasts From the East

Use the flat of the knife to carefully lift the noodles off the board and into the boiling water.

Gently stir the noodles in the boiling water to separate them. The addition of a little oil will also help to keep them separate.

Egg Noodles

Ingredients   Serves 3-4

200g /8oz gluten free bread flour
2 eggs
2 tbsp olive oil + a little more for cooking the noodles
2 tbsp water
Pinch of salt

Place the flour in a bowl and add the salt. Mix the egg, oil, and water together and then stir into the flour. Mix to combine, then, using your hands, press the mix together to make a dough ball.

Wrap the dough in cling film and place in the fridge to rest for 30 minutes.

Once rested, unwrap and place the dough on a suitable surface for rolling (pastry board/worktop). Place a new piece of cling film (about 50cm long) over the dough and begin to roll out to approx. 2mm thick.

Carefully cut fine strips, approx. 2mm wide, across the dough.

Bring a large saucepan of water to the boil. Add a splash of oil to the water and carefully place the noodles into the pan. Using chopsticks or wooden spoon handle, gently stir the noodles to separate them. Cook for 2 minutes.

Drain the noodles and plunge into a bowl of ice cold water. Drain and set aside, they are now ready to add to a recipe or to be stir-fried with a little soy sauce and served as a side dish. This is a little tedious but worth it! It may help to use a ruler for the first cut to give you a guide line.

Alternatively use a pasta machine with a spaghetti attachment.

Shanghai Chow Mein

Ingredients   Serves 4

Gluten-free egg noodles (see recipe)
500g pork loin, cut into fine strips (marinate as below)
Handful of broccoli – tiny florets
Handful of carrots – cut into matchsticks
Handful of green leek leaves – finely sliced
1 green pepper – finely sliced
2tsp ginger paste
2tbsp garlic infused oil
1 tbsp sesame oil
1 tbsp chilli infused oil

Sauce
2tbsp gluten-free soy sauce
2tbsp tomato sauce
2tsp rice wine vinegar
1 tsp sugar
½ tsp Chinese 5 spice

Make the egg noodles, place in boiling water, and cook for 2 minutes. Drain and plunge into ice cold water, drain and set aside.

Heat the oils in a wok. Add the ginger paste and leeks, stirring until the leeks begin to soften. Add the meat to the wok and stir-fry for 5 minutes. Pour the contents of the wok into a warm bowl and set aside.

Using more oil, if required, stir-fry the noodles for 5 minutes. Remove and set aside in a separate bowl.

Heat the pan again with a splash more of oil and add the vegetables. Stir-fry for 2 minutes. Place the pork back in the wok with the vegetables, add the sauce, and stir well. Add the noodles, stir through, and serve.

See recipe for egg noodles...

Using a pasta machine, roll to finest and cut into fine noodles

Marinate the pork after slicing:
3 tbsp gluten-free soy sauce
2 tbsp Mirin

Aromatic Crispy Duck

Ingredients   Serves 2

2 duck legs
75g/3oz potato flour

Marinade
½ tsp Chinese 5 spice
½ tsp cinnamon
½ tsp ginger
2 tbsp rice wine or dry sherry
1 tbsp homemade chilli sauce (see recipe)
1 tbsp gluten-free light soy sauce
2 tbsp brown sugar
1 tbsp garlic infused oil

Combine the marinade ingredients together and rub into the duck legs. Place in a glass dish, cover with cling film and leave in the fridge to marinate overnight.

Preheat the oven to Gas Mark 4/180C.

Remove the duck from the marinade and place in a roasting tin, skin side up. Roast until the skin is golden and crispy – approximately 10 minutes. Turn the oven up to Gas Mark 7/220C. Roast for a further 5 minutes. Remove from the oven and allow the duck to rest for a few minutes. Slice the duck into bite size pieces and dust all over with the potato flour. Shake off any excess flour.

Use a deep-fat fryer or, carefully, heat a half-full wok with vegetable oil.

Carefully place the duck pieces, in small batches, into the hot oil and fry until crisp. Remove with a slotted spoon and place on kitchen paper to drain.

Serve immediately.

Test the oil temperature with a cube of bread; it should sizzle and turn golden in 15 seconds.

Serve with pickled salad (see recipe).

Egg Fried Rice

Ingredients   Serves 4

400ml /15floz long grain rice
800ml /1½ pint water
1 tbsp vegetable oil
2 small eggs, beaten
3 spring onion greens, chopped
Gluten-free Soy Sauce
Salt and Pepper

Put the rice and the water into a large saucepan and salt. Bring the rice to the boil, stir once then reduce the heat and simmer for approximately 15 minutes. Test the rice; it should be tender and fluffy. Drain the small amount of water that is left and leave to cool.

Heat the oil in a large frying pan or wok and add the egg and the spring onion greens. Scramble the egg as it cooks. Add the cold rice and stir-fry until piping hot. Splash on a little soy sauce, stir and serve.

Rice rules!

Twice the water than the rice.

Hoisin sauce

Ingredients

120ml /4floz soy sauce
3 tblsp soft brown sugar
1 tsp garlic infused oil
¼ tsp toasted sesame oil
1 tsp chilli infused oil
2 tsp rice vinegar
3 tsp Mirin
60ml /3½floz water
3 tsp thickening granules/cornflour

Mix all the ingredients together in a small saucepan. Stirring constantly, heat until boiling begins. Reduce the heat and simmer for 10-15 minutes. Pour into a small serving dish and leave to cool.

As it cools it will thicken. If the sauce is not thick enough, it can be returned to the heat to reduce further or more thickening granules can be added.

Use on mandarin pancakes or as a dip with vegetable croutons and prawn crackers.

If you use cornflour, when returning to the heat to thicken more, you must let the sauce simmer for 5 minutes to allow the cornflour to cook out.

Mandarin Pancakes

Ingredients   Serves 6

450g /1lb gluten-free plain flour (and a little more for dusting the work surface)
10ml/2 tsp xanthan gum
350-375ml/12-13floz boiling water
15ml /1 tblsp cold water
10ml/2tsp sesame oil

Sift the flour into a large mixing bowl.   Gradually pour in the boiling water. Using a wooden spoon, stir vigorously until well mixed and then add the cold water. It should be like bread dough. When cool enough to handle, knead lightly until soft and smooth. Cover with a cloth and leave to stand for 20-30 minutes.

Place the dough on a floured board or work surface. Divide in half and knead until smooth again. Using both hands, roll each half into a sausage shape (40cm/16 in long). Divide each roll equally into 16 pieces, 32 in total.

Clear the board or work surface and place a piece of cling film on the top. Lightly brush the cling film with sesame oil. One at a time, stand a piece of dough upright on the cling film and squash with the palm of your hand, brush with oil. Place another piece of cling film on top of the dough. Using a rolling pin, roll the dough out to about 15-16cm / 6-6½ in. Set aside. Repeat with all 32 pieces.

Heat an unoiled heavy frying pan or flat griddle over a medium to low heat. Place as many pancakes as will fit into the pan. Fry for 1-2 minutes, or until light spots start to appear. Turn over to cook the other side; they will quickly puff up, indicating that they are done.

Remove from the pan and repeat with the rest of the pancakes. Set the cooked pancakes on a plate and cover with a cloth to prevent them drying out.

Steam the pancakes for 5-10 minutes in a wok or steamer before serving.

Try to avoid using too much flour as the pancakes will become floury.

Using cling film stops the dough from sticking and reduces the risk of using too much flour.

Spread with hoisin sauce, add thin strips of cucumber and spring onion greens along with Aromatic Crispy Duck or Pulled Pork and roll up!

Sticky Spare Ribs

Ingredients   Serves 4-6

750g Pork spare ribs

Marinade

6 tbsp tamarind sauce
8 tbsp Tomato Ketchup
½ tsp garlic infused oil
½ tsp chilli infused oil
2tbsp soft brown sugar
1 tsp Chinese 5 spice
4 tbsp gluten free soy sauce

Pre-heat the oven to Gas 2 /150C.

Place all marinade ingredients together in a large bowl and stir well. Use to coat spare ribs. Leave to marinate for at least 2 hours.

Remove the ribs from the marinade and place in a roasting pan. Pour any residue marinade over the ribs. Cover with tin foil and bake in the oven, on the bottom shelf for approximately 2 hours.

Heinz Tomato Ketchup contains no onion or garlic.

This marinade can also be used for pork chops or duck breasts; lower the oven temperature to Gas 1/140C

Sweet & Sour Pork

Ingredients   Serves 4

500g diced pork
1 bunch spring onion greens, chopped
2 peppers, chopped (1 red, 1 green or yellow)
1 432g can pineapple pieces in natural juice
½ tsp asafoetida
1 tbsp garlic infused oil
½ tbsp chilli infused oil

Sauce
Tomato sauce
1 tbsp brown sugar
½ tsp English mustard powder
2 tbsp white wine vinegar
½ tsp Chinese 5 spice
Salt and pepper to taste

Drain the pineapple juice into a measuring jug and set the pineapple pieces aside. Add the tomato sauce; the combination of juice and tomato sauce should be 350ml. Stir in the remaining ingredients and season.

Heat the oils in a wok or large pan, add the asafoetida, stir, and then add the spring onion greens; fry for 2 minutes. Add the diced pork and fry to brown. Stir in the sauce, pineapple, and peppers. Cook on a medium heat and bring to the boil. Reduce the heat and simmer for 20-30 minutes.

If you like the peppers with more crunch, add them 10 minutes before you are ready to serve.

Oriental Pulled Pork

Ingredients   Serves 6-8

750g pork leg
4oz water

Basting paste

½ tsp cayenne pepper
3 tsps Chinese 5 spice
1 tsp ground ginger
½ tsp asafoetida
1 tsp salt
3 tsps dark soy sauce

Pre-heat the oven to Gas 2/150C.

Place the meat on a trivet, in a deep roasting tin. Mix the basting ingredients together and rub into the meat. Pour the water into the tin, around the meat. Cover tightly with foil and cook for ¾ hour, turn the heat down to Gas 1/140C and cook for 4 hours.

Transfer to a serving plate and use forks to pull the meat apart.

Alternatively use a whole duck.

Serve with Hoisin sauce and mandarin pancakes or gluten free wraps.

Oriental Pulled Pork on a gluten free wrap with Hoisin Sauce,
chopped spring onion greens and cucumber.

Cut a large wrap into quarters and secure with a cocktail
stick for ready assembled starters or canapes.

Pickled Salad

Ingredients

½ cucumber, sliced in half lengthways and deseeded
100g/4oz radish,
1 red chilli, de-seeded
1 tblsp rice vinegar
½tsp rice wine or dry sherry
½tsp salt
1 tsp sugar
1 tbsp fresh coriander leaves, finely chopped

Cut the cucumber and radish into mini matchsticks. Finely chop the red chilli. Place in a bowl and add the remaining ingredients. Stir well. Cover with cling film and refrigerate for 1 hour.

Serve with a twist of milled salt and a sprinkle of dried chillies (optional).

Teriyaki Pork Kebabs

Ingredients   Serves 4-6

500g diced pork
1 red pepper, cut into 1in pieces
1 tin cubed pineapple, drained
1 large courgette,
12 skewers (if wooden – soak for 30 minutes before assembling the kebabs)

Marinade

3 tbsp gluten-free Soy Sauce
3 cloves of garlic, halved (to be discarded with the marinade)
1 tbsp garlic infused oil
1 tbsp chilli infused oil
Pinch of dried chillies
A few grinds of Black pepper

Basting sauce

400ml /14 floz water
1 tsp Bovril
2 tsp chopped fresh ginger
2 tbsp gluten-free Soy Sauce
2 tbsp cornflour
2 tbsp brown sugar
3 tsp lime juice
Pinch dried chillies
1 tbsp agave nectar

Place all the marinade ingredients together in a large bowl and mix well. Add the pork and stir, ensuring the meat is well coated. Place in the fridge and leave to marinate for at least 30 minutes, preferably overnight.

Place all the basting ingredients together in a saucepan, stir, and bring to the boil. Reduce the heat and leave to simmer until it has reduced by approx. 1/3. Stir occasionally. Remove from the heat and set aside to cool, whilst you assemble the kebabs.

Remove the meat from the marinade, and begin to thread the kebab ingredients onto the skewers; courgette, pepper, pork pineapple; repeating until the skewer is full and leaving enough space to handle each end of the skewer. Make sure the ingredients are tightly packed.

Using a pastry brush, baste the kebabs with the sauce, turning to cover all sides.
Place on the barbeque, griddle, or under the grill, turning to ensure even cooking and basting each turn. Cook for 15-20 minutes, or until meat is cooked through.

The basting sauce can be made the day before use and kept in the fridge.

It may need heating a little before use.

Sweet Chilli Sauce

Ingredients

3 cloves of garlic, cut in half
180ml/6floz water
3 chillies, roughly chopped
60ml/2floz white wine vinegar
125g/2 ½oz sugar
½tsp salt
16g / 2 sachets arrowroot
2 tbsp water

Pour the water into a saucepan, add the garlic, and place on a high heat. Bring to a rolling boil. Turn the heat off and leave for 5 minutes to infuse plenty of garlic flavour.

Remove the garlic cloves and pour the infused water into a blender along with the chillies, vinegar, sugar, and salt. Blend until the chillies are finely chopped.

Transfer the liquid back to the saucepan and bring to the boil. Lower the heat and simmer for about 10 minutes.

Combine the arrowroot with the 2 tblsp water and whisk into the chilli mixture. Continue to simmer for 2 minutes, whilst stirring.

Remove from heat and leave to cool; it will thicken more as it cools. Transfer to a sterilized jar and refrigerate.

The garlic is used to infuse the water. Remember to discard them!

Depending how hot you like to go, leave the chilli seeds in or deseed some or all of them!

Side Dishes

Potato Rosti

Ingredients   Makes 10-12

4 large potatoes, peeled
Salt and pepper
3-4tblsp vegetable oil

Grate the potatoes on the 'cheese' side of the grater. Place in a clean tea towel and squeeze out all the excess water over the sink.

Place the potato into a bowl and season well.

Heat the oil in a large frying pan. When hot, add a tablespoon of potato mixture to the frying pan, gently flattening the rosti with a fish slice. Add more to fit the pan and fry for 2 minutes each side.

Remove from the pan and place on a piece of kitchen paper to absorb some of the oil.

Just before you are ready to serve them, reheat the oil (you may need to add a little more oil)and pop the rosti back into the pan for 1 minute each side or until they are crispy on the outside.

Alternatively place in a hot oven (Gas 8/230C) to finish.

Rustic Potato Wedges

Ingredients   Serves 3-4

4 large potatoes, peeled
Garlic infused spray oil
4tbsp gluten free plain flour
Salt and pepper
1tsp dried thyme
3-4tblsp vegetable oil

Pre-heat the oven to Gas Mark 8/230C.

Cut the potatoes into thick wedges. Place in a roasting tray and spray lightly with the garlic infused oil.

Place the flour in a plastic bag and season with salt and pepper and the thyme. Add the potatoes and shake well, ensuring the potatoes are well coated with the flour mix.

Take the potatoes out of the bag and place back into the roasting tin. Drizzle the vegetable oil over the wedges and place in the oven for 30 minutes or until cooked and crispy.

Dauphinoise Potatoes

Ingredients   Serves 2

175g/6oz peeled, thinly sliced potatoes
½ tsp garlic infused oil
175ml/6floz lactose-free cream
Salt and pepper
10g/½oz margarine

Preheat the oven to Gas 2/150C.

Rub the garlic infused oil around a small ovenproof dish. Layer the potato slices into the dish, seasoning as you go. Pour over the cream and dot the butter on the top.

Bake in the oven for 1½ hours, turn the heat up to Gas 8/220C for the last 10 minutes to brown.

Alternatively place the dish under the grill to brown.

Ratatouille

Ingredients   Serves 3-4

1 aubergine, diced
2 courgettes, sliced
1 bunch spring onion greens, chopped
1 tin chopped tomatoes
Salt and pepper
1 tbsp garlic infused oil
1 tsp dried basil

Heat the oil in a large saucepan and stir-fry the spring onion greens until soft. Add the aubergines and courgettes and stir for 1 minute.

Pour in the tinned tomatoes and dried basil. Season and bring to the boil. Lower the heat to a gentle simmer and cook for 30 minutes, stirring occasionally.

Leek Greens in Cheese Sauce

Ingredient   Serves 4

4 leeks- green part only, sliced

Cheese sauce
300ml /10floz lactose-free milk
25g/1oz margarine
25g/1oz gluten-free plain flour
50g/2oz cheddar cheese, grated (plus a little more to sprinkle on the top)
Pinch dried English mustard
Salt and pepper

Melt the margarine in a saucepan and stir in the flour and mustard. Keep over the heat and stir to form a smooth paste. Add the milk slowly, stirring constantly until the sauce begins to boil. Add the cheese and continue stirring until it comes back to boil. Add the seasoning, simmer, and stir for 2 minutes. The sauce should now be smooth and creamy.

Bring a saucepan of water to the boil. Add the leek greens and cook for 2-3 minutes. Drain well and transfer to an ovenproof dish.

Pour the cheese sauce over the leek greens and sprinkle with the extra cheese.

Place under the grill until the top is golden brown.

Pickled Red Cabbage

Ingredients

500g/1lb 2oz red cabbage (about a ¼ of a large head)
4tbsp sea salt
½ tsp black peppercorns
2 bay leaves
1 rosemary sprig
500ml/18floz red wine vinegar
400g/14oz castor sugar
1 bunch spring onion greens, finely chopped

Remove the core and thinly slice the red cabbage. Place in a large bowl and add the sea salt. Wrap the peppercorns, bay leaves, and rosemary in a small piece of muslin, tie securely, and then crush the bag to release the flavours. Add this to the cabbage. Stir well and set aside for 1 hour. Stir after ½ hour.

To make the pickling liquid, pour the red wine vinegar, sugar, and spring onion greens into a saucepan. Add 50ml/2floz water, stir and bring to the boil. Remove from the heat and leave to cool.

Remove the spice bag from the cabbage and place it in the pickling liquid.

Rinse the cabbage well with cold running water to remove the salt. Place in a colander and leave to drain for 10 minutes. Wrap the cabbage in a clean tea towel and squeeze out any excess water.

Transfer the cabbage to a large sterilized Kilner jar. Pour the pickling liquid in, seal and set aside for at least 1 hour.

The cabbage will keep for up to a month in the refrigerator.

Makes a great side dish, at a moment's notice.

<u>Sterilizing glass jars.</u>

Pre-heat the oven to Gas 3/160C. Wash the jars with hot soapy water and rinse. Whilst still wet, stand the jars upside down on a baking tray and place in the oven for 20 minutes.

Take care not to touch the inside of the jar when turning them upright.

Green Beans with Chilli & Mustard seeds

Ingredients   Serves 4

450g/1lb French green beans
4tbsp garlic infused olive oil
1tbsp whole black mustard seeds
½ fresh chilli (deseeded if desired), finely chopped
1tsp salt
½ tsp sugar
Ground black pepper

Bring a pan of water to the boil and drop in the green beans. Boil rapidly for 3-4 minutes. Drain and immediately rinse under cold, running water. Set aside.

Heat the oil in a large frying pan. When hot add the mustard seeds. As soon as they begin to pop, add the chilli and fry for a few seconds.

Add the beans, sugar, and salt. Stir and reduce the heat to medium/low. Stir-fry for 6-7 minutes. Grind some black pepper over the beans and transfer to a warm serving dish.

This is a traditional side dish for Indian meals but also works well with grilled or roasted meats.

Tomato Salsa

Ingredients

1 tin chopped tomatoes, well drained
½ bunch spring onion greens, finely chopped
½ tsp dried chillies or 1 fresh chilli (deseeded if desired), finely chopped
Juice of ½ lime or lemon
1 tbsp fresh coriander, finely chopped
1 tsp fresh parsley, finely chopped
1 tbsp garlic infused oil
Salt and pepper

Place all ingredients together in a medium sized bowl and mix well.

Transfer to a serving bowl.

Great with Teriyaki Kebabs or as a dip with nachos.

Pasta in Tomato Sauce

Ingredients   Serves 2-3

150g Gluten free pasta and 200ml boiling water

<u>Sauce</u>
500g passata
200ml water
1/2 tsp salt
½ tsp dried basil
¼ tsp asafoetida
1 tbsp olive oil
1 tbsp soft brown sugar
1 tsp white wine vinegar

Heat the oil and add the asafoetida and stir. Add the remaining sauce ingredients, stir, and bring to the boil. Turn the heat down and simmer gently for 30minutes.

Add the pasta of your choice and 200ml water. Bring back to the boil and cook until the pasta is al dente (about 10-15 minutes depending on the pasta shape). Stir frequently.

This is the nearest thing to tinned spaghetti that I've found!

A very useful accompaniment to sausages and mash!

Make the sauce and freeze it for a quick dish of spaghetti on toast when you need something fast and easy!

Yorkshire Pudding

Ingredients Makes 4

110g/4oz gluten free self-raising flour
142ml/4floz lactose-free milk
Pinch of salt
1 egg
1 tsp vegetable suet

2 tsps vegetable oil (for cooking)

Preheat the oven to Gas 7/220C.

Place all the ingredients in a bowl and beat until smooth.

Pour the oil into individual Yorkshire pudding tins or deep bun tins and heat in a When the oil is hot, carefully pour the batter in. Cook for about 20 minutes.

Try not to open the oven door whilst the Yorkshire puddings are cooking as this may make them sink.

These freeze really well. Remove from the oven and cool before freezing. Place in a hot oven from frozen for 5 to 10 minutes.

Dumplings

Ingredients   Makes 4-6

100g /4oz gluten-free plain flour
30g /1½ oz margarine
½ tsp baking powder
Pinch of salt
¼ tsp mixed dried herbs
Lactose-free milk to mix

Place the flour and baking powder in a bowl and mix well. Add the margarine and rub together until you get a crumble. Stir in the seasoning and herbs.

Add enough milk to make the mix stick together and form a soft dough.

Using a dessert spoon, add spoonful's of dough to the top of your favourite stew about 20-25 minutes before the end of the cooking time.

Herb Stuffing

Ingredients

- 250g/9oz fresh gluten-free breadcrumbs
50g/2oz gluten-free vegetable suet (optional)
1 tbsp fresh parsley, chopped
1tbsp fresh sage, chopped
1 tbsp fresh thyme, chopped
½ bunch spring onion greens, finely chopped
2 tsp lemon juice
1 egg
Salt and pepper

Place all the ingredients together in a large bowl. Mix well.

Use as an alternative to stuff chicken/turkey/goose (neck end only) or divide into balls and cook in the roasting tin with the meat for the last 30 minutes of the meat cooking time.

Curry Paste

Ingredients

3tbsp coriander seeds
2tbsp cumin seeds
1tbsp mustard seeds
1tsp fennel seeds
1tsp black peppercorns
1tsp ground turmeric
1tsp ground cinnamon
1tsp paprika
¾ tsp dried chillies (a little more for a hotter kick!)
1tsp salt
3tsp ground ginger
1tbsp tomato puree
4tbsp white wine vinegar
1tsp garlic infused oil
Vegetable oil to cover paste for storing

Put the seeds and peppercorns in a dry frying pan and roast over a medium heat for approximately 3 minutes, stir until the mustard seeds begin to pop. Remove from the heat and set aside to cool.

Once cool, grind the roasted mixture to a fine powder; use an electric grinder or pestle and mortar. Add remaining dry ingredients and mix well.

Add the tomato puree and white wine vinegar and mix to a paste.

Use immediately or store in sterilised jar; cover the paste with vegetable oil and seal the jar. Keep in the refrigerator for up to 1 week.

Chip Shop Curry Sauce

Ingredients

3tsp butter or margarine
3tsp gluten free plain flour
2tsp curry paste (see recipe)
500ml/18floz Chicken stock
3tbsp lactose-free milk
1tsp sugar
1tbsp sultanas (optional)

Melt the butter or margarine in a saucepan over a medium heat. Stir in the flour and curry paste and cook for 1 minute.

Gradually add the stock, stirring continuously. Raise the heat to high and bring the liquid to a boil. Lower the heat again until the liquid is simmering gently. Add the milk, sugar, and sultanas (if using). Stirring frequently, simmer until the sauce is smooth and creamy.

Fish and chips from the chip shop are a welcome easy meal!
Many now have the option of gluten free batter.

My son missed the curry sauce; so here is my version! It freezes well, so pour any leftovers into an ice-cube tray and freeze. Reheat in a microwave for an instant accompaniment.

Onion Gravy

Ingredients   Serves 2

1 bunch spring onion greens, chopped
1 tsp butter
275ml /10floz homemade stock
1 tsp Bovril
1 tsp gravy browning
½ tsp fresh thyme
1-2 tbsps thickening granules
Salt and pepper

Heat the butter in a saucepan and fry the onion greens until soft. Add the water, Bovril, gravy browning and herbs. Stir and bring to the boil. Reduces the heat and simmer for 10 minutes. Stir in the thickening granules until you have the consistency you prefer. Season with salt and pepper.

Serve with sausages, toad in the hole, or liver and mashed potatoes.

If you have cooked sausages or liver, then use this pan to make your gravy for added flavour.

Onion Jam

Ingredients

3 bunches spring onion greens, finely chopped
60ml /2floz olive oil
2 sprigs fresh parsley, finely chopped
2 bay leaves
1 sprig of fresh rosemary, finely chopped
110g /8oz granulated sugar
350ml /6 floz white balsamic vinegar
¼ tsp salt
1 tbsp agave nectar

Heat the oil in a saucepan and add the spring onion greens and herbs, cook until beginning to brown (about 5 minutes over a medium heat).

Pour in the sugar and agave nectar, do not stir! Cook for 5 minutes, until the sugar melts. Turn the heat up and cook, without stirring, to caramelise (approximately 6 minutes).

Stir in the white balsamic vinegar, lower the heat and simmer for approximately 5 more minutes, until the jam is thick. Stir in the salt and set aside to cool slightly.

This jam will keep in the fridge for 5 days.

Best served warm or at room temperature.

Tomato Chutney

Ingredients

2 tbsp garlic infused oil
1 bunch spring onion greens, finely chopped
½ small fresh chilli (deseeded if desired)
800g /1lb 12oz ripe tomatoes, evenly chopped with core removed.
200ml red wine vinegar
275g /10oz granulated sugar
2 tbsp fresh coriander, finely chopped
Salt and pepper

Heat the oil in a large saucepan and add the spring onion greens and chilli. Fry until soft.

Add the remaining ingredients. Bring to the boil, stirring constantly. Reduce the heat to medium and simmer gently for approximately 1 hour, until thick. The chutney is thick enough when you pass a wooden spoon across the bottom of the pan and the jam separates showing the bottom of the pan.

Allow to cool slightly before pouring into sterilised jars and seal with lids. Store sealed jars at room temperature for up to 3 months.

Once opened, store in the fridge and use within 5 days.

Mint and Coriander Yoghurt

Ingredients

100g lactose-free natural yoghurt (see recipe)
1 tbsp fresh coriander, finely chopped
1 tbsp fresh mint, finely chopped
1 tsp lime juice

Place all ingredients together in a medium sized bowl and mix well. Cover and place in the fridge for at least 1 hour before serving to allow flavours to release into the yoghurt.

Remove from the fridge, stir, and transfer to a serving bowl.

Great with Chicken Tikka or Seekh Kebabs

Naughty But Nice Puds

Strawberry Cheesecake

Ingredients   Serves 4-6

Base
75g /3oz margarine, melted
175g /6oz gluten free digestive biscuits/oat cookies, crushed

Topping
2 tins strawberries
1 tbsp agave nectar
1 level tsp gelatine

Filling
300g /11oz Cottage cheese
225g/ 8oz ricotta cheese
2 x 125g tubs lactose-free strawberry yoghurt
4 tbsp lemon juice
4 eggs, separated
4 level tsp gelatine
75g /3oz sugar

Combine the margarine and biscuits and press into a 15cm / 6 in deep tin. Put in the fridge until needed.

Place the cottage and ricotta cheeses, yoghurts, and lemon juice in a blender and blend until smooth.

Whisk the egg yolks with the sugar until thick and pale. Add the cheese mix and whisk to combine.

Sprinkle the 4 tsp gelatine over 4 tbsp hot water, place over a pan of boiling water and stir to dissolve. Whisk into the yolks and cheese mixture.

In a large, clean bowl, using clean whisks, whisk the egg whites to stiff peaks and then fold into the cheese mixture. Pour over the biscuit base and return to the fridge to set.

Drain one of the tinned strawberries and put into a saucepan with the other whole tin. Bring to the boil, reduce the heat, and simmer to reduce the liquid by half. Add the agave nectar and stir. Sprinkle the gelatine onto the strawberry mix and stir well. Leave to cool slightly before pouring over the cheesecake.

Lactose-free cream cheese can be used instead of ricotta if preferred.

Lemon Meringue Pie

Ingredients   Serves 4-6

Pastry
225g /8oz gluten free plain flour
175g /6oz butter
45g /1¾oz icing sugar
1 large egg
1 tsp cold water

Topping
4 egg whites
225g /8oz castor sugar
2 tsp cornflour

Filling
6 wax-free lemons, zest and juice
65g /2½oz cornflour
250g /9oz castor sugar
6 egg yolks
450ml /16floz boiling water

Pastry: Blend the flour and butter to a fine crumbly texture, stir in the sugar and make a well in the middle of the mixture.

Beat the egg and water together and pour into the well. Stir to combine, using your hands, bring the pastry together to form a ball. Cover and place in the fridge to rest for 20-30 minutes.

Pre-heat the oven to Gas 4/180C.

Remove the pastry from the fridge and roll out to approximately 3mm thick and transfer to a 24cm /9in deep pie tin. Trim the sides slightly higher than the side of the tin to allow for shrinkage and place a sheet of baking parchment and beans inside (uncooked rice works just as well) to stop the pastry from puffing up.

Bake in the oven for 15 minutes. Remove the beans and bake for a further 5 minutes. Set aside and reduce the oven temperature to Gas 2/150C.

Filling: Mix the lemon juice, zest and cornflour to a paste in a small bowl. Pour the water into a saucepan and bring back to the boil. Add the lemon mix and stir continuously until thick. Remove from the heat.

Place the egg yolks and sugar in a large bowl and whisk until thick and pale. Carefully whisk in the lemon mixture. Set aside for a few minutes to cool then pour into the pastry case.

Topping: In a large, clean bowl, whisk the egg whites to soft peaks. Add the sugar, a little bit at a time, until all the sugar is added and the mixture is stiff and glossy. Sprinkle on the cornflour and whisk to mix.

Spoon the meringue on top of the pie, covering all the lemon filling. Swirl your spoon over the top and place in the oven to bake for 15 minutes. The filling should be set and the meringue golden and crisp.

Strawberry Shortcake

Ingredients

350g/12oz gluten-free self-raising flour
125g/4oz margarine
125g/4oz castor sugar
100ml /4floz lactose-free milk
1 egg
250ml /10floz lactose-free cream, whipped
300g /10-12oz fresh strawberries, cut into quarters or sliced

Pre-heat the oven to Gas 4/180C.

Rub the margarine and flour together to make fine breadcrumbs. Stir in the sugar and mix well. Beat the egg and the milk together and add to the dry mix. Stir to a soft dough.

Press into 2 lined and greased 18cm/6in sandwich tins.

Bake in the oven for 15 to 20 minutes. When the shortcake begins to loosen from the sides of the tin and the centre springs back when lightly pressed, it is ready to take out of the oven.

Turn out onto a wire rack to cool before filling with lactose-free cream and fresh strawberries.

Alternatively, make individual cakes, using 9cm / 3½in baking tins.

Rhubarb Crumble

Ingredients   Serves 4

1 batch sweet crumble (see recipe)
2tsp ground ginger

1kg /2lb rhubarb, cut into pieces
50g /2oz demerara sugar
2 tbsp orange juice

Pre-heat the oven to Gas 4/180C.

Mix the ground ginger into the crumble mix.

Pour the mix onto a baking tray and spread out. Place in the oven for 10 minutes. Remove from the oven and set aside.

Place the rhubarb in a baking dish and sprinkle over the sugar and orange juice. Cover with the crumble.

Bake in the oven for 45 minutes. The crumble should be golden and crisp.

Chocolate Orange Mousse

Ingredients   Serves 4-6

1 sugar-free orange jelly
150ml/¼ pt boiling water
50g plain chocolate, melted
250ml/ 9floz lactose-free cream
200ml/7floz lactose-free milk

Dissolve the jelly in the water and set aside. Whisk the cream and milk together until it is light and bubbly.

Pour the hot jelly into chocolate and mix. Add to the whisked cream and mix well.

Transfer the mousse into one large bowl or divide into ramekin dishes and place in the fridge to set.

These also look good served in coffee cups or wine glasses.

Grate some orange zest on top to decorate.

Raspberry Roulade

Ingredients   Serves 6

3 eggs
75g /3oz castor sugar
¼ tsp xanthan gum
75g /3oz gluten free plain flour
250ml lactose-free cream, whipped
30g broken meringue pieces
½ tsp vanilla paste (optional)
300g fresh raspberries

Pre-heat the oven to Gas 6/200C

Place the eggs and sugar into a large bowl and whisk until mouse like. Gently sift the flour and xanthan gum together and fold into the mixture. Take care not to over mix.

Pour into a greased and lined 18 x 28 cm/7 x 11in swiss roll tin. Bake in the oven for 8-10 minutes. Check the cake is cooked by gently pressing the centre, it should spring back.

Lay a damp tea towel on the work surface and place a piece of sugared, greaseproof paper on top. Turn the cake out onto the paper and carefully peel off the lining paper. Press your finger along one of the short edges making a flattened 1 cm strip. Starting with this edge, roll the cake up with the paper rolling with it. Leave to cool.

Stir the vanilla paste, if using, into the stiff, whipped cream. Unroll the cake and fill with cream, meringue, and raspberries. Roll up carefully, without the paper.

If you are whisking by hand, stand the bowl over a pan of hot water

Treacle Tart

Ingredients   Serves 4-6

225g /8oz rich shortcrust pastry (see recipe)

600g /1lb 5oz golden syrup
185g /6½ oz fresh, gluten free bread crumbs
1 tsp ground ginger
1 lemon, juice and zest

Pre-heat the oven to Gas 5/190C

Line a 20cm /8in pie tin with the pastry and blind bake (prick the base or use baking beans) for 15 minutes in the pre-heated oven.

Meanwhile, pour the golden syrup into a saucepan and heat gently, but do not boil. Stir in the bread-crumbs, ginger, lemon zest and juice. Mix together until the breadcrumbs are well coated.

Pour into the pastry case and return to the oven for 30-40 minutes. Serve with lashings of custard!

Sticky Toffee Pudding

Ingredients   Serves 4-6

200g /7oz gluten-free self-raising flour
125g /4oz soft brown sugar
Pinch of salt
125ml /4floz lactose-free milk
2 eggs
6 tbsp butter, melted
2 tsp vanilla extract
¼ tsp mixed spice (optional)
¼ tsp ground cinnamon (optional)

Sauce

125g /4oz butter
200g /7oz soft brown sugar
250ml /9floz lactose-free cream

Preheat the oven to Gas 3/170C

Sift the flour into a large bowl. Add the salt and sugar and mix well.

In another bowl, mix the eggs with the melted butter and lactose-free milk. Stir in the vanilla extract, mixed spice, and cinnamon (if using). Whisk until frothy.

Pour the liquid mixture into the dry ingredients and mix to a smooth batter. Transfer in to a greased 20cm/8in square cake tin and bake in the oven for 25-30 minutes.

Sauce

Add the butter, sugar, and cream together in a saucepan. Over a medium heat, bring to a simmer, stirring constantly until thick. Remove from heat and allow to cool slightly before serving.

Lemon Sorbet

Ingredients

15 wax-free lemons
275g /10oz granulated sugar
Ice cold water

Finely gate the rind of 2-4 lemons and place in a saucepan.

Squeeze the juice from all the lemons and place in a measuring jug to find the quantity of juice (make a note of this!). Pour the juice into a saucepan with the zest. Add the sugar and place over a medium heat, stirring until the sugar has dissolved. Leave to cool.

Measure an equal quantity of water as the juice and stir into the cooled juice.

Pour into an ice-cream maker and churn until smooth and semi-frozen. Transfer the sorbet into a freezer-proof tub and place in the freezer until firm.

Or

Pour into a freezer-proof tub and place in the freezer. Stir every half hour to prevent crystals forming. Repeat until sorbet is firm.

An ice-cream maker is ideal for this but it can also work without one.
It just takes a bit more effort!

The more zest the more zing!

Remove from the freezer for a few minutes before serving.

Mum's Rhubarb & Jelly Pie

Ingredients   Serves 6

1 batch of rich shortcrust pastry (see recipe)
700g /1½lb rhubarb, cut into 1in pieces
1 strawberry jelly
1 tsp castor sugar

Pre-heat the oven to Gas 6/200C.

Roll out just over half of the pastry between 2 pieces of cling film and line a 23cm /9in pie dish. Place a piece of greaseproof paper gently over the pastry and fill with baking beans or rice. Blind bake in the oven for 10 minutes.

Carefully lift the greaseproof paper, with the beans/rice off the pastry. Place the rhubarb in the pie, standing the pieces up, fitting in as many pieces as you can.

If you are using powdered jelly, sprinkle it over the top of the rhubarb; if using cubed jelly, cut it into small pieces and scatter across the rhubarb.

Roll out the remaining pastry, again between the cling film, and place over the pie. Carefully press the two layers of pastry together around the edge using your thumbs and fore fingers to create a scalloped effect. Make a small hole in the middle of the pie to allow the steam to escape.

Sprinkle with sugar. Return to the oven and bake for 45 minutes. The pastry should be golden and crisp.

Leave the pie to cool before putting in the fridge to set.

Serve cold with lashings of whipped lactose-free cream!

Make this the day before you want to eat it as it needs to set and be eaten cold.

This recipe is dedicated to my mum.

When I was a child pudding was always known as 'wait and see pie' (if you asked what was for pudding the answer was 'wait and see') and when it turned out to be rhubarb jelly pie it was certainly worth waiting for!

Lactose-free Natural Yoghurt

Ingredients

1 ltr Lactose-free UHT milk
1-2 tsp natural live yogurt for your first batch /1-2 tsp homemade lactose-free yoghurt for future batches

Electric yoghurt maker

Follow the direction for your specific yoghurt maker.

Natural yogurt is very low in lactose so the small amount needed to make your first batch will be further reduced by means of dilution by the new yoghurt.

Make your next batch within 3 days, for best results, with your homemade yoghurt.

The whey that separates from the yoghurt is great for making bread.

Salted Caramel Sauce

Ingredients

220g /7oz granulated sugar
90g /3½ oz butter, cubed
120ml /4floz lactose-free cream
1 tsp salt

Heat the sugar gently, to melt. The sugar will clump together, eventually melting into a golden brown liquid. Avoid burning the sugar.

As soon as the sugar has melted, add the butter and beat well. Be aware that the caramel may bubble and spit.

Drizzle in the cream, stir and bring to the boil. Continue to boil for 1 minute. Remove from the heat; add salt, stir and leave to cool.

This will keep for up to 2 weeks in an air tight jar in the fridge or for a day at room temperature.

Warm slightly before using in a recipe.

Cakes & Biscuits

Victoria Sponge Cake

Ingredients

125g/4oz margarine
125g/4oz castor sugar
2 eggs
75g/3oz gluten free self-raising flour
25g/1oz cornflour
1 tsp xanthan gum

Pre-heat the oven to Gas Mark 4/180C.

Cream the margarine and sugar together until light and fluffy. Beat in the eggs, one at a time.

Sift the flours and the xanthan gum together and add to the batter mix. Using a metal spoon, carefully fold the flour in until the batter is smooth.

Pour into 2 lined and greased 18cm/6in sandwich tins.

Bake in the oven for 15 to 20 minutes. When the sponge cake begins to loosen from the sides of the tin and the centre springs back when lightly press the cake is ready.

Turn out onto a wire rack to cool before filling with jam or butter cream.

**If you add a little of the flour whilst beating in the eggs, it will help
to stop the mixture from curdling.**

Makes 12 fairy cakes or 9 larger cupcakes.

All In One Chocolate Cake

Ingredients

125g/4oz margarine
125g/4oz castor sugar
2 eggs
75g/3oz gluten free self-raising flour
25g/1oz cornflour
1 rounded tbsp cocoa powder
1 tsp xanthan gum
1 tsp baking powder
20ml lactose-free milk

Pre-heat the oven to Gas Mark 4/180C.

Sift the flours, cocoa and baking powders, and the xanthan gum together into a large mixing bowl. Add the remaining ingredients and beat until well mixed.

Pour into 2 lined and greased 18cm/6in sandwich tins.

Bake in the oven for 15 to 20 minutes. When the sponge cake begins to loosen from the sides of the tin and the centre springs back when lightly press the cake is ready.

Turn out onto a wire rack to cool before filling with butter cream.

An electric whisk is ideal for a quick and easy mix!

Chocolate Swiss Roll

Ingredients

3 eggs
125g/4oz castor sugar
25g/1oz cocoa
¼ tsp xanthan gum
50g/2oz gluten free plain flour
1 tblsp hot water

Pre-heat the oven to Gas Mark 6 / 200C.

Place the eggs and sugar into a large bowl and whisk until mouse-like. Gently sift the flour, cocoa, and xanthan gum and fold into the mixture with the hot water. Take care not to over mix.

Pour into a greased and lined 18 x 28 cm/7 x 11 in swiss roll tin. Bake in the oven for 8-10 minutes. Check the cake is cooked by gently pressing the centre; it should spring back.

Lay a damp tea towel on the work surface and place a piece of sugared, greaseproof paper on top. Turn the cake out onto the paper and carefully peel off the lining paper. Press your finger along one of the short edges, making a flattened 1 cm strip. Starting with this edge, roll the cake up with the paper rolling with it. Leave to cool.

Unroll the cake and fill with cream or buttercream; re-roll without the paper.

If you are whisking by hand, stand the bowl over a pan of hot water.

Chocolate Marble Cake

Ingredients

175g/6oz margarine
175g/6oz castor sugar
3 eggs
135g/4 ½oz gluten free self-raising flour
40g/1 ½oz cornflour
1 tsp xanthan gum
1 tsp baking powder
55g/2oz plain chocolate
55g/2oz white chocolate

Filling
Salted caramel (see recipe), approximately half the quantity

Topping
75g/3oz plain chocolate
Knob of butter
25g/1oz white chocolate

Pre-heat the oven to Gas Mark 3/170C.

Place all the cake ingredients, except the chocolate, into a large bowl and beat until smooth and creamy.

Melt the plain and white chocolate separately.

Split the cake batter equally into 2 bowls. Add the plain chocolate to one and the white chocolate to the other.

Place an alternate spoonful of plain and white mixture into 2 greased and lined 20cm/8in sandwich tins. Using a skewer (or the handle of a wooden spoon) swirl through the mixture.

Bake in the oven for 40 to 45 minutes. When the sponge cake begins to loosen from the sides of the tin and the centre springs back when lightly pressed, the cake is ready. Turn out onto a wire rack to cool.

Once the cake has cooled down, spread the salted caramel onto one half of the cake.

Melt the plain chocolate and beat in the butter. Spread on the second half of the cake. Place this half on top of the salted caramel.

Melt the white chocolate and pour it on the top of the cake, to decorate.

You can also use a narrow knife to test if the cake is cooked. Push the blade through the centre of the cake, if it comes out clean, the cake is ready.

Basic Buttercream

Ingredients   Fills a medium sized cake or tops 12 fairy cakes

140g/5oz butter or margarine, softened
280g/10oz icing sugar
1 tbsp lactose-free milk
A few drops of vanilla extract (optional)

Beat the margarine until soft and pale. Add half the sugar and blend till smooth. Add the remaining sugar and 1 tbsp of the milk and mix again until light and fluffy.

Chocolate Buttercream

140g/5oz butter or margarine, softened
280g/10oz icing sugar
40g/1½oz cocoa powder, sifted
2tbsp lactose-free milk

Coffee Buttercream

140g/5oz butter or margarine, softened
280g/10oz icing sugar
2 tsp coffee granules (dissolved in 1 tbsp boiling water)

Lemon Buttercream

140g/5oz butter or margarine, softened
280g/10oz icing sugar
2 tsp lemon juice

When making the chocolate buttercream, sift the icing sugar and cocoa powder together.

Kids love to decorate their own cupcakes!

Lemon Drizzle Cake

Ingredients

Cake

125g/4oz margarine
125g/4oz castor sugar
2 ½ large eggs
75g/3oz gluten free self-raising flour
25g/1oz cornflour
1 tsp xanthan gum
1 tsp baking powder
Grated zest of a lemon

Drizzle crunch

50g/2oz granulated sugar
Juice of ½ a lemon

Pre-heat the oven to Gas Mark 4/180C.

Sift the flours, xanthan gum, and the baking powder together. Add the remaining cake ingredients.

Beat until smooth.

Pour into a greased and lined 18cm/7in square tin.

Bake in the oven for 35-40 minutes.

When the sponge begins to loosen from the sides of the tin and the centre springs back when lightly pressed, the cake is ready. Leave it in the tin whilst you make the drizzle crunch.

Mix the sugar and lemon juice together and pour over the warm cake.

Leave to cool before turning out and enjoying!

For a more golden coloured sponge, replace the castor sugar for demerara sugar.

Butter Biscuits

Ingredients   Makes 15

75g/3 oz butter
25g/1oz castor sugar
25g/1oz Demerara sugar
125g/4oz gluten-free self-raising flour
25g/1oz corn flour
Pinch salt
¼ tsp xanthan gum

Pre-heat the oven to Gas Mark 3/170C.

Cream the butter and sugars until smooth. Sift the flours, salt, and xanthan gum together and add to the butter mix. Mix well. Form into a ball then roll into a thick sausage, about 5cm/ 2 inches in diameter. Wrap tightly in cling film and place in the fridge for 30 minutes.

Remove from the fridge and carefully cut the roll into 1cm slices. Place on a lightly oiled baking trays. Bake in the oven for 12 minutes. Swap shelves, turn, and bake for a further 3 minutes.

Remove to a cooling rack. Leave to cool.

Cover with foil if the biscuits are beginning to brown.

**Try them with sugar (cinnamon flavoured is good), sprinkled on whilst
still hot or coat with chocolate when cooled.**

Millionaire's Shortbread

Ingredients

Biscuit base

175g/6oz unsalted butter or margarine
75g/3oz castor sugar
200g/7oz gluten free plain flour
50g/2oz cornflour

Caramel

225g/8oz unsalted butter or margarine
125g/4oz castor sugar
4 tbsp golden syrup
250ml lactose-free cream
50ml lactose-free milk

Topping

200g/7oz plain chocolate
25g/1oz unsalted butter or margarine

Pre-heat the oven to Gas 4/180C.

Begin with the biscuit base. Cream the butter and sugar together until light and creamy. Add the flour and cornflour; stir until the mixture begins to bind together. With your hands, gently knead the mixture to a smooth dough.

Line a 23cm/9in square cake tin with baking parchment. Press the biscuit dough into the base, ensuring it is level, and smooth the top with the back of a spoon. With a fork, prick the biscuit all over.

Bake in the oven for 25 to 30 minutes. Remove from the oven and set aside to cool in the tin.

Place all the caramel ingredients in a saucepan and stir over a medium heat to dissolve the sugar. Slowly bring the caramel to a boil, then cook for 5-7 minutes, stirring constantly. When thick and golden-brown, turn off the heat and allow to cool slightly. Pour over the biscuit base and leave to cool completely.

Put the chocolate in a bowl and melt over a pan of simmering water. Stir frequently until the chocolate has melted. Stir in the butter and spread evenly across the caramel. Set aside to set.

Cut into fingers or squares.

Chocolate Biscuits

Ingredients   Makes approximately 15

125g/4oz margarine
25g/1oz icing sugar
125g/4oz gluten-free self-raising flour
½ tsp xanthan gum
Pinch of salt
2 tbsp cocoa powder
A few drops of vanilla essence
2 tsp lactose-free milk

Pre-heat the oven to Gas Mark 5/190C.

Beat the margarine and icing sugar together.
Sift the flour, xanthan gum, salt and cocoa into the mixture. Add the vanilla essence and milk. Stir in and beat until creamy.
Transfer mixture into a piping bag with a 2.5cm (1 in) fluted nozzle, and pipe fingers, approx. 7.5cm (3 in), well apart on a baking tray lined with non-stick paper.

Bake in the oven for 15-20 minutes.

Cool on a wire rack.

I use an icing bag to pipe the mixture onto baking trays but if you prefer you can use a teaspoon. Give each biscuit a heaped tsp, slightly flatten the top.

Check the biscuits after 10 mins and turn the tray around. Cook until just firm; they will crisp up on cooling.

Oaty Cookies

Ingredients   Makes 18

4 packets Quakers Oat So Simple, Golden Syrup
125g/4oz soft brown sugar
1 tsp xanthan gum
50g/2oz gluten free plain flour
120ml/4floz vegetable oil
1 egg
75g/3oz sultanas/raisins (optional)

Preheat the oven to Gas Mark 3/170C.

Mix the oats, flour, xanthan gum, and oil together. Set aside for 20 minutes.

Beat the egg thoroughly and add to the mix. Stir well.

Form into small balls and place on lightly oiled baking sheets, slightly spaced apart. Dip a fork into water and gently squash each ball.

Bake in the oven for 15-20 minutes. Leave on the baking trays for 2-3 minutes then remove to a wire rack. Leave to cool.

Add the sultanas/raisins with the egg if you are adding them.

Lemon Crisps

Ingredients   Makes approximately 30

125g/4oz margarine
225g/8oz castor sugar
1 egg
Zest of 1 lemon
Juice of 1 lemon
¾ tsp vanilla extract
½ tsp baking powder
¼ tsp bicarbonate of soda
275g/10oz gluten free plain flour

<u>Icing</u>

100g/4oz icing sugar
1 tbsp lemon juice

Pre-heat the oven to Gas 3/170C.

Beat the margarine and sugar together until light and creamy. Add the lemon zest, juice, and vanilla extract.

Sift the flour, baking powder, and bicarbonate of soda into the mixture. Stir in the wet ingredients and beat until just combined.

Drop rounded teaspoons of mixture, 3cm/1½in apart, on a baking tray lined with non-stick paper.

Bake in the oven for 10-12 minutes. Leave to cool for 1 minute on the baking tray before transferring to a wire rack.

Mix the icing sugar and lemon juice to a thick pouring consistency. Spoon into a piping bag with a small nozzle and decorate each biscuit with zigzag lines. Set aside to set.

Basics

Béchamel Sauce

Ingredients

1 ltr lactose-free milk
75g/3oz margarine
75g/3oz gluten-free plain flour
½ bunch spring onion greens, chopped
1 bay leaf
2 sprigs fresh parsley
Salt and pepper

Pour the milk into a saucepan; add the herbs and spring onion greens. Bring to the boil then remove from the heat. Pour into a jug and allow to infuse for 30 minutes before straining.

Put the butter into the saucepan, gently melt, making sure it does not go brown or burn. Stir in the flour. Beat the roux until it is smooth. Gradually pour in the infused milk, stirring continuously with a wooden spoon, allowing all the milk to be incorporated before adding more milk. When about half the milk has been added, use a whisk to ensure a smooth sauce and add the remaining milk in larger amounts. Bring to the boil and stir until the sauce thickens. Season.

White Sauce

Ingredients

1 ltr lactose-free milk
75g/3oz margarine
75g/3oz gluten-free plain flour
Salt and pepper

Put the butter into the saucepan, gently melt, making sure it does not go brown or burn. Stir in the flour. Beat the roux until smooth. Gradually pour in the milk, stirring continuously with a wooden spoon, allowing all the milk to be incorporated before adding more milk. When about half the milk has been added, use a whisk to ensure a smooth sauce and add the remaining milk in larger amounts. Bring to the boil and stir until the sauce thickens. Season.

Homemade Stock

Ingredients

Left-over bones from the Sunday roast
2 carrots
1 bunch spring onion greens
1 sprig fresh rosemary
2 sprigs fresh thyme
5 sprigs fresh parsley
2 bay leaves
Ground pepper

Place all the ingredients in a large saucepan and add enough cold water to cover. Bring to the boil and reduce heat to allow the stock to simmer for 3-4 hours. Strain through a fine sieve and leave to cool.

When cooled, pour into ice cube trays and freeze until required.

> **Using a raw carcass will give a deeper flavour and a clearer stock.**
>
> **If you do not have fresh herbs, add a bought bag of bouquet garni instead.**
>
> **When freezing, ice cube bags are useful as they won't spill in the freezer!**

Shortcrust Pastry

Ingredients

250g/8oz gluten-free plain flour
50g/2oz lard
50g/2oz margarine
Pinch salt
2 tbsp cold water

Rub the fats into the flour until it resembles fine breadcrumbs. Stir in the salt. Add the water and mix to a soft dough. Form into a ball and place in the fridge to rest for 20 minutes.

Place a piece of cling film onto a pastry board or work surface and put the pastry ball in the centre. Squash the dough to a thick flat disc with the palm of your hand. Put another piece of cling film on top of the pastry. Using a rolling pin, roll the pastry to the required size.

Too much water will make the pastry tough.

Gluten-free pastry is very crumbly and difficult to pick up, so using the cling film helps the rolling and transfer to a pie dish.

Remove the top layer of cling film and place the dish upside down on the pastry. Holding the cling film and the dish in place, quickly flip it over. Gently ease the pastry into the dish and make the necessary repairs around the side.

Rich Shortcrust Pastry

Ingredients

250g/8oz gluten-free plain flour
125g/4oz margarine
Pinch salt
1 tsp sugar
1 egg, beaten
 Cold water to mix (if needed)

Place the flour and margarine in a large bowl and rub together with your fingertips until it resembles fine breadcrumbs. Stir in the salt and sugar. Add the egg and mix to form a soft dough. Add some water (a teaspoonful at a time) if the mix will not come together. Form into a ball, cover, and place in the fridge to rest for 30 minutes.

Place a piece of cling film onto a pastry board or work surface and put the pastry ball in the centre. Squash the dough to a thick flat disc with the palm of your hand. Put another piece of cling film on top of the pastry. Using a rolling pin, roll the pastry to the required size.

Too much water will make the pastry tough.

As with gluten-free shortcrust pastry, this is very crumbly and difficult to pick up so use the method in the shortcrust recipe to roll out.

Rough Puff Pastry

Ingredients

375g/13oz gluten free plain flour
350g/12oz unsalted butter
Pinch of salt
180ml iced water

Cut the butter into 1cm cubes and place in the freezer for one hour.

Put the flour and salt into a large bowl and add the butter. Using your fingertips, work the butter and flour together until the butter starts to soften at the edges. Pour in the iced water and mix until the flour has absorbed all the water.

Turn out onto a marble slab or work top. Knead to bring together. Place between or cover with parchment paper or cling film and roll out. Roll gently from the centre out and not the edges.

Fold the bottom third over to the middle, then the top third on top. Rotate ¼ turn clockwise (1 turn completed). Repeat rolling, folding and turning until you have completed 4 turns.

Cover and place in the fridge to rest for 30 minutes.

Sweet Crumble

Ingredients

150g /5oz gluten-free plain flour
75g /3oz margarine
75g /3oz sugar
½ tsp of cinnamon or mixed spice (optional)

Pre-heat the oven to Gas 4/180C.

Place the flour and sugar in a bowl and stir. Add the margarine and rub together until combined to look like breadcrumbs. Stir in the spices if desired.

Fill an ovenproof bowl with your favourite fruit, cover with crumble and bake in the oven for 40 minutes.

Can be made in advance and frozen at this stage.

For a crunchier crumble without a soggy bottom, put the crumble mix onto a baking tray and bake in the oven for 10 minutes.

Whilst still hot, pour onto the fruit and bake as usual.

Cover with foil when golden brown.

Savoury Crumble

Ingredients

150g /5oz gluten-free plain flour
75g /3oz margarine
Salt and pepper
½ tsp mixed herbs (optional)

Place the flour in a bowl and season. Add the margarine and rub together until combined to look like breadcrumbs. Stir in the herbs if desired.

Use as an alternative to a pastry topping to a meat pie. Follow the recipe cooking instructions.

Custard

Ingredients

350ml/12floz lactose-free milk
50ml/2 floz lactose-free cream
2 large egg yolks
1½tbsp cornflour
100g castor sugar
½tsp vanilla extract

Put the milk and cream into the saucepan and gently bring to near boiling point.

Meanwhile, whisk the cornflour, yolks, sugar, and eggs together in a large bowl. Continue whisking whilst gradually adding the hot milk mixture.

Wipe out the saucepan and pour the custard back into it. Return to the heat, stir constantly with a wooden spoon, until thick.

Delicious hot or cold!

Food Chart

When using the Low FODMAP diet, you should ensure that you get a healthy balance of nutrients. The following chart identifies foods with high, medium, and low levels of FODMAPs along with portion sizes where appropriate.

The aim of the lifestyle diet is not to exclude FODMAPs but to lower your intake/avoid the problem foods. Some people may tolerate certain high FODMAP foods and have problems with other low or moderate foods.

**Please seek advice from your doctor or dietician
for specific allergy or dietary requirements.**

FOOD CHART

	Quantity	Go	Beware	Stop!
VEGETABLES				
Alfalfa	125 grams	Go		
Artichoke, globe	½ small			Stop!
Artichoke, hearts, canned in water & vinegar	60 grams		Beware	
Artichoke, hearts, canned in water & vinegar	1 tablespoon	Go		
Artichoke, Jerusalem				Stop!
Asparagus	2 spears			Stop!
Aubergine	125 grams	Go		
Bean sprouts	125 grams	Go		
Bamboo shoots	80 grams	Go		
Beans, broad	125 grams			Stop!
Beans, green	10 beans	Go		
Beetroot	4 slices			Stop!
Beetroot	2 slices	Go		
Bok choy	250 grams	Go		
Broccoli	250 grams			Stop!
Broccoli	125 grams	Go		
Brussel Sprouts	2 sprouts	Go		
Butternut Squash	125 grams		Beware	
Cabbage, common and red	250 grams	Go		
Cabbage, Savoy	250 grams			Stop!
Carrot	9 slices	Go		
Cauliflower	125 grams			Stop!
Celeriac	½ celeriac	Go		
Celery	Less than 5cm stalk	Go		
Chicory leaves	125 grams	Go		
Chilli	Small	Go		
Chives	1 tablespoon	Go		
Choy sum	250 grams	Go		
Cucumber	125 grams	Go		
Courgette	125 grams	Go		
Endive leaves	4 leaves	Go		
Fennel leaves	125 grams	Go		
Fennel bulb	125 grams	Go		
Garlic	1 clove			Stop!

Ginger root	1 teaspoon	🟩
Kale	250 grams	🟩
Leek, white part	1	🟧
Leek, greens (leaves)	125 grams	🟩
Lettuce	250 grams	🟩
Mushroom	250 grams	🟧
Okra	3 pods	🟩
Onion, Spanish, shallot, white	1/4 onion	🟧
Onion, spring, white bulb (Scallions)	125 grams	🟧
Onion, spring green leaves only (Scallions)	1 bunch	🟩
Peas, snow/sugar snap/ Chinese	10 pods	🟧
Peas, garden, thawed	125 grams	🟧
Peas, garden, thawed	60g	🟩
Peppers, (Capsicum)	125 grams	🟩
Potato	1 medium	🟩
Potato, sweet	250 grams	🟧
Potato, sweet	125 grams	🟩
Pumpkin	125 grams	🟩
Radish	2	🟩
Silver beet	250 grams	🟩
Spinach, baby	250 grams	🟩
Squash	2 squash	🟩
Sweet corn	1/2 cob	🟩
Tomato, canned	125 grams	🟩
Tomato, cherry, common	125 grams	🟩
Turnip		🟩
Water Chestnuts	125 grams	🟩
Processed Vegetables		
Seaweed	125 grams	🟩
Tomatoes, sundried	2 tablespoons	🟨
FRUIT		
Apple	1 medium	🟧
Apricot	2 medium	🟧
Avocado	1/4 whole	🟧
Banana, common, firm/ripe	1 medium	🟩
Banana, sugar, firm	1 medium	🟩
Banana, sugar, ripe	1 medium	🟧
Blackberry	10 berries	🟧
Blueberry	20 berries	🟩
Cherries	6	🟧

Cherries	3	
Custard Apple	125 grams	
Dragon fruit	1 medium	
Grapefruit	½ medium	
Grapes	20	
Kiwi fruit	1 medium	
Lemon juice	1 teaspoon	
Lychee	10	
Mandarin	1	
Mango	½	
Melon, Cantaloupe	125 grams	
Melon, Honeydew	125 grams	
Melon, watermelon	250 grams	
Nectarine	1 medium	
Orange	1 medium	
Passion fruit	1 whole pulp	
Paw Paw	125 grams	
Peach	1 medium	
Pear	1 medium	
Persimmon	1 whole	
Pineapple	125 grams	
Pomegranate	125 gm or 1 small	
Rambutan	4	
Raspberry	10 berries	
Rhubarb	½ stalk	
Strawberry	8 medium	
Tamarillo	2	
Processed Fruit		
Apple, dried	3 rings	
Apricots, dried	4	
Banana, dried	10 chips	
Coconut milk	125 millilitres	
Coconut, dried (desiccated)	125 grams	
Coconut, dried (desiccated)	60 grams	
Cranberries, dried	2 tablespoons	
Dates, dried	4	
Figs, dried	4	
Pear, dried	6 pieces	
Prunes, dried	4	

PROTEIN & VEGITARIAN SUBSTITUTES		
Meat e.g. Beef, Pork, Lamb	125 grams	
Chicken, turkey	125 grams	
Fish	125 grams	
Eggs	2	
Quorn, mince	75 grams	
Tempeh	150 grams	
Tofu, plain	250 grams	
DAIRY & DAIRY SUBSTITUES		
Milk, (cow's) full fat, semi-skimmed, skimmed	125 millilitres	
Milk (goat's)	125 millilitres	
Milk, Lactose-free	250 millilitres	
Milk, evaporated	125 millilitres	
Milk, sweetened, condensed	80 millilitres	
Milk, coconut, canned	125 millilitres	
Milk, coconut UHT	125 millilitres	
Milk, coconut UHT	240 millilitres	
Milk, almond	250 millilitres	
Milk, oat	30 millilitres max	
Milk, rice	200 millilitres	
Milk, soya, (soya bean)sweetened/unsweetened	125 millilitres	
Milk, soy (soy protein)	250 millilitres	
Buttermilk	125 millilitres	
Cream, single, double, whipping, extra thick	50 millilitres	
Cream, sour	50 millilitres	
Cream, Lactose-free	50 millilitres	
Custard, regular, low fat	125 millilitres	
Ice cream, vanilla	2 level scoops (90g)	
Ice cream, lactose-free	2 level scoops (90g)	
Yoghurt, natural, regular, low fat	85 millilitres	
Yoghurt, flavoured, regular, low fat	85 millilitres	
Yoghurt, Lactose-free, natural,	170 millilitres	
Yoghurt, Lactose-free, strawberry, raspberry,	170 millilitres	
Yoghurt, soya (soya bean)	85 millilitres	
Yoghurt, soy (soy protein)	85 millilitres	
Cheese		
Brie	40 grams	

Camembert	40 grams	🟩
Cheddar	40 grams	🟩
Cottage cheese	4 tablespoons (36g)	🟩
Cream cheese	4 tablespoons (36g)	🟨
Edam	40 grams	🟩
Feta	125 grams	🟩
Goats cheese	60 grams	🟩
Mozzarella	60 grams	🟩
Parmesan	60 grams	🟩
Quark	40 grams	🟩
Ricotta	80 grams	🟨
Ricotta	40 grams	🟩
MEAT & MEAT SUBSTITUES		
Meat	125 grams	🟩
Chicken	125 grams	🟩
Fish	125 grams	🟩
Eggs	2	🟩
Quorn mince	75 grams	🟩
Vegetarian mince	75 grams	🟥
Tempeh	150 grams	🟩
Tofu, plain	150 grams	🟩
Sausages	1	🟥
Sausages, Gluten Free, no onion or garlic	2	🟩
Chorizo	1 slice	🟥
Processed meat (check ingredients)		🟥
CEREAL/CEREAL PRODUCTS		
Breakfast Cereals		
All Bran	1 tablespoon	🟥
Bran flakes	1 tablespoon	🟥
Cornflakes, plain	25 grams	🟨
Cornflakes, plain, Gluten Free	25 grams	🟩
Muesli, plain	50 grams	🟥
Muesli, Gluten Free	50 grams	🟥
Oats	50 grams	🟨
Oats	25 grams	🟩
Quinoa flakes	150 grams	🟨
Rice, puffed or popped	25	🟩
Rice, puffed or popped	12 grams	🟩

205

Any cereal with nuts/dried fruit	25 grams	🟧
Bread		
Gluten Free (no onion/garlic/apple juice)	2 slices	🟩
Naan, plain/garlic & coriander	100 grams	🟧
Naan, plain, Gluten Free	100 grams	🟩
Pumpernickel		🟧
Sourdough - oat	2 slices	🟨
- oat	1 slice	🟩
- rye/dark rye	2 slices	🟧
- spelt	2 slices	🟩
Wheat –White, Wholemeal, Multigrain	2 slices	🟧
Wraps, plain/wholemeal	1	🟧
Wraps, plain/wholemeal, Gluten Free	1	🟩
Grains & Grain products		
Couscous, wheat (cooked)	150 grams	🟧
Couscous, maize (cooked)	150 grams	🟩
Noodles, wheat (cooked)	150 grams	🟧
Noodles, rice (cooked)	150 grams	🟩
Oat Bran	2 tablespoon	🟩
Pasta, Gluten Free (uncooked)	75 grams	🟩
Pasta, quinoa (uncooked)	75 grams	🟩
Pasta, spelt (uncooked)	75 grams	🟩
Pasta, Wheat (uncooked)	75 grams	🟧
Polenta, cornmeal (cooked)	150 grams	🟩
Rice, white/brown/wild (uncooked)	75 grams	🟩
Wheat bran, processed/unprocessed	1 tablespoon	🟧
Pulses & Legumes		
Baked beans	160 grams	🟧
Broad (Fava) beans (cooked)	75 grams	🟧
Butter beans (canned)	75 grams	🟧
Chickpeas (canned)	125 grams	🟨
Chickpeas (canned)	60 grams	🟩
Four Bean Mix	125 grams	🟧
Haricot Beans (cooked)	75 grams	🟧
Lentils, red/green/yellow	75 grams	🟨
Lentils, red/green/yellow (cooked)	35 grams	🟩
Nuts and seeds		
Almonds	20 nuts / 24 grams	🟧
Almonds	10 nuts / 12 grams	🟩

Cashews	10 nuts	■
Chestnuts	5 nuts	■
Hazelnuts	10 nuts	■
Macadamia nuts	10 nut	■
Peanuts	10 nuts	■
Pecans	15 nuts	■
Pistachio	15 nuts	■
Poppy seeds	1 tablespoon	■
Pumpkin seeds	1 tablespoon	■
Sesume seeds	1 tablespoon	■
Sunflower seeds	1 tablespoon	■
walnuts	10 ½ nuts	■
BEVERAGES		
Fruit/vegetable juices		
Apple	1 glass	■
Cranberry	1 glass	■
Orange	1 glass	■
Orange	½ glass	■
Mango		■
Vegetable	1 glass	■
Cordial/Squash		
Apple/berry	1 glass	■
Orange	1 glass	■
Teas & Coffee		
Coffee, white	1 cup	■
Coffee, black or with Lactose-free milk	1 cup	■
Drinking Chocolate	1 cup	■
English Tea, with milk	1 cup	■
English Tea, black or with Lactose-free milk	1 cup	■
Fennel Tea	1 cup	■
Herbal Tea, weak	1 cup	■
Herbal Tea, strong	1 cup	■
Peppermint Tea	1 cup	■
Alcohol		
Beer	375 millilitres	■
Red wine	150 millilitres	■
White wine, dry	150 millilitres	■
White wine, sweet	150 millilitres	■

SPREADS & JAMS		
Bovril	1 teaspoon	
Honey	1 tablespoon	
Marmalade	2 tablespoons	
Strawberry	2 tablespoons	
Mixed berries	2 tablespoons	
Peanut Butter	1 tablespoon	
Vegemite	1 teaspoon	
CHOCOLATE		
Dark	30 grams	
Milk	30 grams	
White	30 grams	
Carob	30 grams	

Appendix

Tips:

- Garlic infused oil can be found in the supermarket. Alternatively you can fry garlic cloves in vegetable oil for a few minutes, then discard the cloves or make a garlic 'tea bag' using a small piece of muslin – wrap the muslin around the cloves and secure with an elastic band or string and use like a bouquet garni to infuse flavour, discarding the 'bag' at the end of cooking (the muslin can be washed and reused).

- Spring onion greens (the green part above the white bulb) or scallions give a good onion flavour. When you cut the green bits off put the white bulbs in a pot of water and grow new green shoots.

- Asafoetida (found in the herb/spice section in the supermarket) gives an onion flavour. Use small amounts (don't be put off by the smell it has in the jar!)

- Doves Farm Foods gluten-free flours have been used in creating these recipes; other flours may have slightly different results due to the mixture of flours used.

- Bovril makes a great beef stock/additional beef flavour. Shop bought stock cubes/granules can be used instead of homemade stock but check the ingredients for gluten, onion and or garlic.

- McDougal's Thickening granules work well as they can be added into a sauce easily. Alternatively you can use cornflour, mixed with a little water and stir into your sauce.

Conversions

All these are approximate conversions, which have either been rounded up or down. Never mix metric and imperial measures in one recipe; stick to one system or the other.

All spoon measurements stated here are level spoons, unless specified otherwise.

Weights

IMPERIAL	METRIC	IMPERIAL	METRIC
½ oz	10 g	6 oz	175 g
¾ oz	20 g	7 oz	200 g
1 oz	25 g	8 oz	225 g
1½ oz	40 g	9 oz	250 g
2 oz	50 g	10 oz	275 g
2½ oz	60 g	12 oz	350 g
3 oz	75 g	1 lb	450 g
4 oz	110 g	1 lb 8 oz	700 g
4½ oz	125 g	2 lb	900 g
5 oz	150 g	3 lb	1.35 kg

Oven Temperatures

GAS MARK	°F	°C
1	275°F	140°C
2	300°F	150°C
3	325°F	170°C
4	350°F	180°C
5	375°F	190°C
6	400°F	200°C
7	425°F	220°C
8	450°F	230°C
9	475°F	240°C

For fan assisted ovens, if you are not able to switch off the fan function, reduce the temperature by 20 degrees or check the manufacturer's handbook.

Volume

IMPERIAL	METRIC
2 fl oz	55 ml
3 fl oz	75 ml
5 fl oz (¼ pint)	150 ml
1 ¾ pint	1 litre
10 fl oz (½ pint)	275 ml
1 pint	570 ml
1 ¼ pint	725 ml
2 pint	1.2 litre
2½ pint	1.5 litre
4 pint	2.25 litres

Dimensions

IMPERIAL	METRIC
⅛ inch	3 mm
¼ inch	5 mm
½ inch	1 cm
¾ inch	2 cm
1 inch	2.5 cm
1¼ inch	3 cm
1½ inch	4 cm
1¾ inch	4.5 cm
2 inch	5 cm
2½ inch	6 cm
3 inch	7.5 cm
3½ inch	9 cm
4 inch	10 cm

IMPERIAL	METRIC
5 inch	13 cm
5¼ inch	13.5 cm
6 inch	15 cm
6½ inch	16 cm
7 inch	18 cm
7½ inch	19 cm
8 inch	20 cm
9 inch	23 cm
9½ inch	24 cm
10 inch	25.5 cm
11 inch	28 cm
12 inch	30 cm

Units of measurement & sizing

Teaspoon (US,UK, CA) is 5 ml (note: abbreviated ‹t› or ‹tsp›)
Dessert spoon (UK) is 10 ml
Tablespoon (US,UK,CA) is roughly 15 ml (note: abbreviated ‹T›, ‹TB›, or ‹tbsp›)
but a tablespoon(AU) is 20 ml.)

American Cup Conversions

AMERICAN	IMPERIAL	METRIC
1 cup flour	5oz	150g
1 cup caster/ granulated sugar	8oz	225g
1 cup brown sugar	6oz	175g
1 cup butter/margarine/lard	8oz	225g
1 cup sultanas/raisins	7oz	200g
1 cup currants	5oz	150g
1 cup ground almonds	4oz	110g
1 cup golden syrup	12oz	350g
1 cup uncooked rice	7oz	200g
1 cup grated cheese	4oz	110g
1 stick butter	4oz	110g

American Liquid Conversions

IMPERIAL	METRIC	AMERICAN
½ fl oz	15 ml	1 tbsp
1 fl oz	30 ml	1/8 cup
2 fl oz	60 ml	¼ cup
4 fl oz	120 ml	½ cup
8 fl oz	240 ml	1 cup
16 fl oz	480 ml	1 pint